LEARN CHINESE
VOCABULARY
FOR INTERMEDIATE

NEW HSK LEVEL 4 VOCABULARY BOOK
MASTER 1000 WORDS IN CONTEXT

Chinese • Pinyin • English

LingLing

www.linglingmandarin.com

My gratitude goes to my wonderful students who study Mandarin with me. You have inspired my writing and provided me with valuable feedback to complete this book. Your support is deeply appreciated!

A special thanks goes to my husband, Phil, who motivated my creation and assisted with editing the book.

Access
FREE AUDIO

SCAN ME

Check the **"ACCESS AUDIO"** chapter for
password and full instructions
(see Table of Contents)

CONTENTS

天 行 健
tiān　xíng　jiàn

君 子 以 自 强 不 息
jūn　zǐ　yǐ　zì　qiáng　bù　xī

As heaven's movement is ever vigorous,
so must a gentleman constantly strive for excellence.

- BOOK OF CHANGES -

INTRODUCTION

Congratulations on successfully completing Levels 1 to 3 of the **NEW HSK Vocabulary Series!** Your hard work has led you to a significant milestone in your learning journey - the Intermediate level. In Level 4, you'll be introduced to 1000 new Chinese words, further enriching your language skills and enabling you to communicate in a wider range of topics.

The NEW HSK Intermediate Levels (4-6) will expand your Chinese vocabulary by over 3000 words, building upon the 2000 words from the Elementary Levels (1-3). Mastering levels 1-6 enables fluent and refined communication, opening doors to numerous opportunities in travel, work, deeper relationships, and personal growth.

WHAT IS THIS BOOK

This book introduces the official HSK 4 vocabulary, presenting 1000 words essential for mastering contemporary Chinese. Designed for intermediate learners, it offers a deeper dive into the nuanced language needed for real-world proficiency, including in formal and business contexts. Whether you're preparing for HSK 4 or seeking to enrich your Chinese skills, this book ensures a practical and effective learning experience with its focus on language application through working examples and coverage of critical grammar and sentence structures.

All the keywords are presented in alphabetical order according to the pinyin, each featuring:

- Simplified Chinese characters used in Mainland China
- Pinyin for pronunciation aid
- English definitions
- Complete sentence examples demonstrating usage
- Full English translations
- Downloadable Chinese audio

BONUS CONTENT

Alongside helping you to master HSK Level 4 vocabulary, this book also includes a special chapter focused on enhancing grammar skills. This chapter covers 20 essential grammar points and widely used sentence structures, incorporating vocabulary from HSK Level 4. This integration ensures a seamless progression from learning individual words to constructing fluent, natural-sounding sentences, mirroring the way native speakers use the language.

HOW THIS BOOK WILL HELP

Effectively learning Chinese involves more than just memorizing isolated words. This book boosts vocabulary retention by providing necessary examples, which help you master not only the words but also their appropriate usage, encompassing common sentence patterns and relevant language.

Study and work with the examples provided, create your own and use them often, focus on incorporating new words into your interactions as frequently as possible, and before long you'll be confidently excelling in your everyday Chinese interactions. Whether or not you plan to take the HSK exam, using and applying the content of this book will enhance your conversational abilities.

LEVEL UP YOUR LEARNING WITH COMPANION BOOKS

I highly recommend complementing your learning with my book **Chinese Conversations for Intermediate**. It will immerse you in authentic everyday scenarios in modern China, enhancing your speaking and listening skills. It will serve as an indispensable companion for anyone aspiring to converse fluently in modern Chinese settings.

If you enjoy engaging stories and want to explore Chinese culture deeper through its legends, myths, and folktales then you should pick up **Chinese Stories for Language Learners: Intermediate**. It provides an entertaining approach to enrich your language skills while delving into the rich tapestry of Chinese cultural narratives.

FREE DOWNLOADABLE AUDIO

Great news! The Chinese audio files for the book is a FREE gift for you, which you can access from the Access Audio page (see table of contents). I strongly encourage you to download and use the audio as part of your learning with this book.

NEW HSK

HSK, short for Hanyu Shuiping Kaoshi (Mandarin Level Examination), is an internationally recognized skill test for non-native Chinese speakers. It is officially introduced by the Chinese government and organized by the Chinese Education Ministry Hanban/Confucius Institutes. The new HSK standard (HSK 3.0) was implemented in July 2021, replacing the old HSK Standard with its 6 levels. The new version features 9 levels, incorporating a more specific classification system, including levels and bands. Compared to its predecessor, the new HSK has been upgraded and expanded, with an increased number of words required for each level.

As a general learner, focusing on levels 1 to 6 will enable you to become an effective Mandarin speaker. Levels 7 and above are specifically designed for advanced learners, such as those intending to pursue Master's or PhD programs in Chinese language studies.

LEARN CHINESE WITH A NEW VISION

The Chinese language, which has evolved over 3500 years, embodies a rich diversity and artistic depth. As one of the most widely spoken languages globally, proficiency in Chinese unlocks a myriad of opportunities in travel, business, and personal development.

Learning Chinese, however, transcends mere language acquisition. It is an immersion into a distinctive cultural mindset and an avenue to broadening your worldview. Immersing yourself in its language and cultural nuances offers a deep appreciation of a heritage that has flourished for millennia.

HOW TO USE THIS BOOK

Here are some tips to use this book most effectively:

1. **Stick to a fixed routine**. For example, master ten words per day or week - you pick a number and schedule that suits you, but most importantly, stick to it.

2. **Capture the Words**. Write down the key vocabulary in a notebook or type it out digitally, this can enhance your memory of the characters.

3. **Read aloud**, especially the sentence examples. Imagine the context in your head when reading.

4. **Test** yourself by covering the Pinyin and English (using a bookmark for example). If you can read and understand the Chinese on its own, you have memorized it.

5. **Listen** to the audio. Practice imitating the audio and keep listening until you can comprehend the audio without the help of the text.

6. **Review** as often as you can. Repetition is the mother of skill!

7. **Create** your own sentence examples. Practice speaking them aloud, and if possible, use them with a language partner. One becomes a true master through creation!

BELIEVE IN YOURSELF

Never be afraid of making mistakes. In real life, even advanced learners and native speakers make mistakes! Learning from mistakes only makes us grow quicker! So, never let mistakes put you off. Instead, be bold, embrace and learn from them!

SET GOALS AND STAY COMMITTED

Have a committed learning attitude and set goals from small to big will lead you to great achievements in your Chinese learning journey. So stay committed and never give up! Just like this Chinese idiom:

| yǒu | zhì | zhě | shì | jìng | chéng |
| 有 | 志 | 者 | 事 | 竟 | 成 |

Nothing is impossible to a willing heart

1

VOCABULARY

IN CONTEXT

1 阿姨 　ā yí

Noun: aunt; polite term to address elder women

wǒ de shū shu hé ā yí yǐ jīng jié hūn nián le
我 的 叔 叔 和 **阿姨** 已 经 结 婚 20 年 了。
My uncle and **aunt** have been married for 20 years.

ér zi qù gěi qīng jié gōng ā yí dào yì bēi shuǐ
儿 子， 去 给 清 洁 工 **阿姨** 倒 一 杯 水。
Son, go to pour a cup of water for the cleaning **lady**.

2 啊 　á

Interjection: expressing doubt or questionning

á tā men tū rán lí hūn le
啊？ 他 们 突 然 离 婚 了？
Ah? They suddenly divorced?

3 矮 　ǎi

Adjective: short (stature)

wǒ mèi bǐ wǒ ǎi yě bǐ wǒ pàng
我 妹 比 我 **矮**， 也 比 我 胖。
My younger sister is **short**er and fatter than me.

4 矮小 　ǎi xiǎo

Adjective: short and small

wǒ shēn cái gāo dà tā shēn cái ǎi xiǎo
我 身 材 高 大， 她 身 材 **矮小**。
My body figure is tall and big, hers is **short and small**.

5 爱国 　ài guó

Adjective: patriotic; love one's country

qū yuán shì zhōng guó gǔ dài wěi dà de ài guó shī rén
屈 原 是 中 国 古 代 伟 大 的 **爱国** 诗 人。
Qu Yuan was a great **patriotic** poet in ancient China.

| 6 | 爱护 | ài hù | **Verb:** to care (out of protection) |

^{wǒ}我 ^{mā}妈 ^{cóng}从 ^{xiǎo}小 ^{jiù}就 ^{jiāo}教 ^{wǒ}我 ^{ài}**爱** ^{hù}**护** ^{dòng}动 ^{wù}物 。

My mother taught me **to care** for animals since I was a child.

| 7 | 安 | ān | **Adjective:** quiet; safe (use with other words)
Verb: to install |

Adj. 这 里 的 环 境 又 **安 静** 又 **安 全** 。
zhè lǐ de huán jìng yòu ān jìng yòu ān quán

The environment here is **quiet** and **safe**.

Verb 公 寓 楼 在 **安** 新 的 供 暖 系 统 。
gōng yù lóu zài ān xīn de gōng nuǎn xì tǒng

The apartment building is **installing** a new heating system.

| 8 | 安置 | ān zhì | **Verb:** to place; to arrange |

他 把 情 人 **安 置** 在 郊 外 的 公 寓 。
tā bǎ qíng rén ān zhì zài jiāo wài de gōng yù

He **placed** his mistress in an apartment in the suburbs.

| 9 | 按时 | àn shí | **Adverb:** on time |

他 对 她 很 好 , 总 是 **按 时** 去 看 她 。
tā duì tā hěn hǎo zǒng shì àn shí qù kàn tā

He treats her well and always go to see her **on time**.

| 10 | 暗 | àn | **Adjective:** dark; dim |

我 的 房 间 **暗** , 但 客 厅 很 亮 。
wǒ de fáng jiān àn dàn kè tīng hěn liàng

My room is **dark**, but the living room is very bright.

11 暗示 àn shì
Verb: to indicate (suggest indirectly)

rú guǒ nǐ shuō cuò, wǒ huì zhǎ yǎn àn shì
如果你说错，我会眨眼暗示。
If you say [something] wrong, I'll wink to **indicate**.

12 巴士 bā shì
Noun: bus

wǒ bù xǐ huān zuò bā shì, yīn wèi tài jǐ le
我不喜欢坐巴士，因为太挤了。
I don't like taking the **bus** because it's too crowded.

13 百货 bǎi huò
Noun: general merchandise

tā shì zhè jiā bǎi huò gōng sī de xīn fù zǒng cái
他是这家百货公司的新副总裁。
He is the new vice president of the department (**general merchandise**) store.

14 摆 bǎi
Verb: to lay (for display)

jiù yào chī fàn le, kuài qù bǎi wǎn kuài
就要吃饭了，快去摆碗筷。
It's time to eat, go **to lay** the dishes.

15 摆动 bǎi dòng
Verb: to wag; to swing

wǒ de gǒu yí kàn dào chī de, jiù bǎi dòng wěi ba
我的狗一看到吃的，就摆动尾巴。
My dog **wags** his tail as soon as he sees food.

16 摆脱 bǎi tuō
Verb: to get rid of

zhè gè zhā nán zài xiǎng bàn fǎ bǎi tuō tā de nǚ péng yǒu
这个渣男在想办法摆脱他的女朋友。
This scumbag is thinking of ways **to get rid of** his girlfriend.

17 败   bài   **Verb:** to fail; to lose

zhè cì xià qí bǐ sài, wǒ men yíng le, tā men bài le
这次下棋比赛，我们赢了，他们**败**了。
In this chess game, we won and they **lost**.

18 办事   bàn shì   **Verb:** to handle affairs/matters (general)

jīng lǐ xǐ huān tā de bàn shì fēng gé
经理喜欢她的**办事**风格。
The manager likes her style of **handling matters**.

19 包裹   bāo guǒ   **Noun:** package; parcel

nǐ kě yǐ zài wǎng zhàn shàng zhuī zōng guó jì bāo guǒ
你可以在网站上追踪国际**包裹**。
You can track international **packages** on the website.

20 包含   bāo hán   **Verb:** to contain

zhè běn shū bāo hán shēng cí hé yǔ fǎ
这本书**包含**生词和语法。
This book **contains** new vocabulary and grammar.

21 包括   bāo kuò   **Verb:** to include

wǒ ài chī de zhōng cān bāo kuò bāo zi、jiǎo zi hé chǎo fàn
我爱吃的中餐**包括**包子、饺子和炒饭。
My beloved Chinese food **includes** steamed buns, dumplings and fried rice.

22 薄   báo   **Adjective:** thin

wǒ mǎi le yí jiàn hòu dà yī hé liǎng jiàn báo chèn shān
我买了一件厚大衣和两件**薄**衬衫。
I bought a thick coat and two **thin** shirts.

5

23 宝   bǎo   **Noun:** treasure

zài zhōng guó, dà xióng māo bèi chēng zuò "guó bǎo"。
在 中 国， 大 熊 猫 被 称 作 " 国 宝 "。
In China, giant pandas are known as "national **treasures**".

24 宝宝   bǎo bao   **Noun:** baby (colloquial)

wǒ men de bǎo bao shì shàng gè yuè chū shēng de
我 们 的 宝 宝 是 上 个 月 出 生 的。
Our **baby** was born last month.

25 宝贝   bǎo bèi   **Noun:** precious; treasured object

zhè gè zuàn shí jiè zhǐ jià zhí wǔ qiān měi yuán, shì gè
这 个 钻 石 戒 指 价 值 五 千 美 元， 是 个
bǎo bèi
宝 贝！
This diamond ring is worth $5000, what a **precious thing**!

26 宝贵   bǎo guì   **Adjective:** valuable

wǒ fā xiàn yǒu qíng bǐ ài qíng bǎo guì
我 发 现 友 情 比 爱 情 宝 贵。
I notice that friendship is more **valuable** than romantic love.

27 宝石   bǎo shí   **Noun:** gemstone

wǒ de dìng hūn jiè zhǐ shì yì kē lán bǎo shí
我 的 订 婚 戒 指 是 一 颗 蓝 宝 石。
My engagement ring is a sapphire (blue **gemstone**).

28 保密   bǎo mì   **Verb:** to keep secret

zhè shì tā de yǐn sī, qǐng nǐ yí dìng yào bǎo mì
这 是 他 的 隐 私 ， 请 你 一 定 要 **保 密** 。
This is his private matter, please **keep** it **secret**.

29 保守   bǎo shǒu   **Adjective:** reserved; conservative

tā yǐ qián hěn bǎo shǒu, xiàn zài hěn kāi fàng
他 以 前 很 **保 守** ， 现 在 很 开 放 。
He used to be **reserved**, now he is open minded.

30 抱   bào   **Verb:** to hug; to cuddle

wǒ ài bào wǒ de gǒu hé māo, yīn wèi tā men tài kě
我 爱 **抱** 我 的 狗 和 猫 ， 因 为 它 们 太 可
ài le
爱 了 ！
I love **to cuddle** my dogs and cats because they are so cute!

31 背景   bèi jǐng   **Noun:** background

qí shí, wǒ bú tài qīng chǔ tā de jiā tíng bèi jǐng
其 实 ， 我 不 太 清 楚 他 的 家 庭 **背 景** 。
Actually, I don't know much about his family **background**.

32 倍   bèi   **Noun:** times (multiple)

tīng shuō tài yáng bǐ yuè liang dà jǐ bǎi bèi
听 说 太 阳 比 月 亮 大 几 百 **倍** 。
I heard that the sun is hundreds of **times** bigger than the moon.

33 被迫   bèi pò   **Verb:** be compelled; be forced

xīn wén jì zhě shuō zǒng tǒng shì bèi pò cí zhí de
新 闻 记 者 说 总 统 是 **被 迫** 辞 职 的 。
News reporters said the president was **forced** to resign.

34 本科   běn kē   **Noun:** undergraduate degree course

tā zài hā fó dà xué dú běn kē zhuān yè shì jīng jì xué
他 在 哈 佛 大 学 读 **本 科** ，专 业 是 经 济 学 。
He is studying an **undergraduate course** at Harvard University, majoring in economics.

35 笨   bèn   **Adjective:** stupid

tā kàn shàng qù hěn bèn qí shí hěn cōng míng
他 看 上 去 很 **笨** ， 其 实 很 聪 明 。
He looks **stupid**, but he is actually very smart.

36 比分   bǐ fēn   **Noun:** score

zú qiú mí men dōu shuō zhè cì de bǐ fēn bù gōng píng
足 球 迷 们 都 说 这 次 的 **比 分** 不 公 平 。
Football fans all say the **score** this time is unfair.

37 毕业   bì yè   **Verb:** to graduate
                                                Noun: graduation

Verb
wǒ men dōu shì qù nián 7 yuè fèn bì yè de
我 们 都 是 去 年 7 月 份 **毕 业** 的 。
We both **graduated** last year in July.

Noun
jiā rén hé péng yǒu men dōu cān jiā le bì yè diǎn lǐ
家 人 和 朋 友 们 都 参 加 了 **毕 业 典 礼** 。
Family and friends all attended our **graduation** ceremony.

38 毕业生　　bì yè shēng　　**Noun:** graduate

很多**毕业生**发现找好工作不容易。
hěn duō bì yè shēng fā xiàn zhǎo hǎo gōng zuò bù róng yì
Many **graduates** find it difficult to find a good job.

39 避　　bì　　**Verb:** to evade; to dodge

你为什么每次看到我都会**避**开？
nǐ wèi shén me měi cì kàn dào wǒ dōu huì bì kāi
Why do you always **dodge** away every time you see me?

40 避免　　bì miǎn　　**Verb:** to avoid

我只是想**避免**跟你吵架。
wǒ zhǐ shì xiǎng bì miǎn gēn nǐ chǎo jià
I just want to **avoid** arguing with you.

41 编　　biān　　**Verb:** to make up (lie); to compile; to compose

为了向朋友借钱，他**编**了很多谎言。
wèi le xiàng péng yǒu jiè qián, tā biān le hěn duō huǎng yán
In order to borrow money from friends, he **made up** many lies.

据说，这首歌是张文**编**的。
jù shuō, zhè shǒu gē shì zhāng wén biān de
It is said that this song was **composed** by Zhang Wen.

42 辩论　　biàn lùn　　**Verb:** to debate
　　　　　　　　　　　　　　Noun: debate

Verb
同学们在教室**辩论**得很激烈。
tóng xué men zài jiào shì biàn lùn de hěn jī liè
The students **debated** fiercely in the classroom.

Noun
这次**辩论**是关于安乐死。
zhè cì biàn lùn shì guān yú ān lè sǐ
This **debate** is about euthanasia.

43 标志   biāo zhì   **Noun:** sign; symbol

wǒ zài qián miàn kàn dào le yí gè tíng chē biāo zhì
我 在 前 面 看 到 了 一 个 停 车 **标 志** 。
I see a car park **sign** ahead.

44 表情   biǎo qíng   **Noun:** expression (facial)

tā kàn dào wǒ shí biǎo qíng fēi cháng jīng yà
他 看 到 我 时 ， **表 情** 非 常 惊 讶 。
When he saw me, his **expression** was very shocked.

45 表扬   biǎo yáng   **Verb:** to praise   **Noun:** praise

Verb

měi cì wǒ nǚ ér zuò fàn wǒ dōu huì biǎo yáng tā
每 次 我 女 儿 做 饭 ， 我 都 会 **表 扬** 她 。
Every time my daughter cooks, I always **praise** her.

Noun

wǒ jué de hái zi xǐ huān fù mǔ de biǎo yáng
我 觉 得 孩 子 喜 欢 父 母 的 **表 扬** 。
I think kids love **praise** from their parents.

46 别   bié   **Adverb:** do not   **Verb:** to pin

Adv.

bié dān xīn tā de shǒu shù fēi cháng chéng gōng
别 担 心 ， 她 的 手 术 非 常 成 功 。
Don't worry, her surgery is very successful.

Verb

tā zài zhì fú shàng bié le yì méi xūn zhāng
他 在 制 服 上 **别** 了 一 枚 勋 章 。
He **pinned** a medal to his uniform.

47 冰   bīng   **Noun:** ice

zài xià tiān wǒ men cháng cháng chī bīng qí lín
在 夏 天 ， 我 们 常 常 吃 **冰** 淇 淋 。
In summer, we often eat **ice** cream.

48 冰箱   bīng xiāng   **Noun:** refrigerator; fridge

wǒ jiā de **bīng xiāng** shì dé guó de míng pái
我 家 的 **冰 箱** 是 德 国 的 名 牌 。
My **refrigerator** is a famous German brand.

49 冰雪   bīng xuě   **Noun:** ice and snow

yǒu yí bù lǎo diàn yǐng jiào **bīng xuě** nǚ wáng
有 一 部 老 电 影 叫 **冰 雪** 女 王 。
There is an old movie called Frozen (**ice and snow** queen).

50 兵   bīng   **Noun:** soldier; force

wǒ de péng yǒu cóng suì jiù kāi shǐ dāng **bīng** le
我 的 朋 友 从 18 岁 就 开 始 当 **兵** 了 。
My friend has been a **solider** since he was 18.

51 并   bìng   **Verb:** to incorporate; to merge
Adverb: actually (for negation)

Verb
zǒng jīng lǐ bǎ xiāo shòu bù mén hé shì chǎng bù mén **bìng** chéng
总 经 理 把 销 售 部 门 和 市 场 部 门 **并** 成
yí gè le
一 个 了 。
The CEO **merged** the sales and the marketing departments into one.

Adv.
duì zhè jiàn shì wǒ de kàn fǎ **bìng** bú zhòng yào
对 这 件 事 , 我 的 看 法 **并** 不 重 要 。
Regarding this matter, my opinion is **actually** not important.

52 不要紧   bú yào jǐn   **Phrase:** never mind; doesn't matter

zhǐ yào nǐ kāi xīn yǒu qián méi qián dōu **bú yào jǐn**
只 要 你 开 心 , 有 钱 没 钱 都 **不 要 紧** 。
As long as you're happy, it **doesn't matter** if you have money or not.

53 不在乎 bú zài hu Phrase: not to care

yǒu shí hòu, wǒ de nán péng yǒu bù zài hu wǒ de gǎn shòu
有时候，我的男朋友**不在乎**我的感受。
Sometimes, my boyfriend **doesn't care** about my feelings.

54 不管 bù guǎn Conjunction: no matter; regardless

bù guǎn tā zěn me jiě shì, wǒ jiù shì bù xiāng xìn
不管他怎么解释，我就是不相信。
No matter how he explained it, I just didn't believe it.

55 不然 bù rán Conjunction: otherwise; why not (suggestion)

bié gēn tā chǎo, bù rán nǐ huì gèng nán guò
别跟他吵，**不然**你会更难过。
Don't argue with him, **otherwise** you'll be even more upset.

kàn lái nǐ men de máo dùn hěn dà, bù rán fēn shǒu ba
看来你们的矛盾很大，**不然**分手吧。
It seems that you have great conflicts, **why not** break up.

56 布置 bù zhì Verb: to decorate; to assign work Noun: decoration

Verb
wǒ zài bāng fù mǔ bù zhì tā men de xīn jiā
我在帮父母**布置**他们的新家。
I'm helping my parents **decorate** their new home.

Noun
tā men duì wǒ de bù zhì fēi cháng mǎn yì
他们对我的**布置**非常满意。
They are very satisfied with my **decoration**.

57 步行 bù xíng Verb: to walk; to go on foot

cóng zhè 'r bù xíng dào shāng chǎng, yào fēn zhōng
从这儿**步行**到商场，要20分钟。
It takes 20 minutes to **walk** to the mall from here.

58 擦　　cā　　**Verb:** to wipe

wǒ qù xǐ wǎn， nǐ kě yǐ bāng wǒ cā zhuō zi ma
我 去 洗 碗， 你 可 以 帮 我 擦 桌 子 吗？

I'm going to wash the dishes, can you **wipe** the table for me?

59 才　　cái　　**Adverb:** only; just
Noun: ability; talent
(use with other words)

Adv.
zhè tào xī zhuāng dǎ zhé hòu， cái liǎng bǎi měi yuán
这 套 西 装 打 折 后， 才 两 百 美 元。

After the suit was discounted, it was **only** two hundred dollars.

Noun
wǒ fēi cháng xīn shǎng tā de cái néng hé cái huá
我 非 常 欣 赏 他 的 才 能 和 才 华。

I really appreciate his **ability** and **talent**.

60 材料　　cái liào　　**Noun:** materials

zhè xiē jīn shǔ cái liào shì cóng zhōng guó jìn kǒu de
这 些 金 属 材 料 是 从 中 国 进 口 的。

These metal **materials** are imported from China.

61 财产　　cái chǎn　　**Noun:** asset; fortune; property

tā dǎ suàn qù shì hòu bǎ cái chǎn juān gěi cí shàn jī gòu
他 打 算 去 世 后 把 财 产 捐 给 慈 善 机 构。

He plans to donate his **fortune** to charity after his death.

62 财富　　cái fù　　**Noun:** wealth

tā shì měi guó de shǒu fù， yōng yǒu jù dà cái fù
他 是 美 国 的 首 富， 拥 有 巨 大 财 富。

He is the richest man in America and has huge **wealth**.

63 采访   cǎi fǎng   **Verb:** to interview (media)
Noun: interview

Verb
rú guǒ nǐ yào cǎi fǎng tā bì xū xiān yù yuē
如果你要**采访**他，必须先预约。
If you want to **interview** him, you must make an appointment first.

Noun
bú guò wǒ tīng shuō tā hěn shǎo jiē shòu méi tǐ de cǎi fǎng
不过，我听说他很少接受媒体的**采访**。
However, I heard that he rarely accepts **interviews** from the media.

64 参考   cān kǎo   **Noun:** reference

qǐng gěi wǒ tuī jiàn yì běn shí yòng de cān kǎo shū
请给我推荐一本实用的**参考书**。
Please recommend me a practical **reference** book.

65 参与   cān yù   **Verb:** to participate
Noun: participation

Verb
jǐng chá shuō tā cān yù le zhè cì móu shā
警察说他**参与**了这次谋杀。
Police say that he **participated** in this murder.

Noun
tā de cān yù ràng shòu hài zhě de jiā rén fēi cháng bēi tòng
他的**参与**让受害者的家人非常悲痛。
The victim's family was devastated by his **participation**.

66 操场   cāo chǎng   **Noun:** playground

nǐ kàn hái zi men zhèng zài cāo chǎng shàng tī zú qiú
你看，孩子们正在**操场**上踢足球。
You see, the children are playing football on the **playground**.

67 操作 cāo zuò

Verb: to operate (machines)
Noun: operation

Verb

jiào liàn zài jiāo xué yuán men rú hé cāo zuò fēi jī
教练在教学员们如何操作飞机。
The instructor is teaching the trainees how **to operate** the aircraft.

Noun

tā shuō zhǎng wò zhèng què de cāo zuò fāng fǎ shì guān jiàn
他说掌握正确的操作方法是关键。
He said mastering the correct method of **operation** is the key.

68 测 cè

Verb: to survey; to measure

wǒ xū yào yòng yì bǎ chǐ zi cè yí xià shā fā
我需要用一把尺子测一下沙发。
I need to use a ruler to quickly **measure** the sofa.

69 测量 cè liáng

Verb: to survey; to measure
Noun: measurement

Verb

wǒ yào cè liáng kè tīng de cháng dù hé kuān dù
我要测量客厅的长度和宽度。
I want **to measure** the length and width of the living room.

Noun

zhè bǎ chǐ zi de cè liáng jié guǒ zhǔn què ma
这把尺子的测量结果准确吗？
Is the **measurement** result of this ruler accurate?

70 测试 cè shì

Verb: to test
Noun: test; examination

Verb

lǎo shī xiǎng cè shì wǒ men de tīng lì shuǐ píng
老师想测试我们的听力水平。
The teacher wants **to test** our listening ability.

Noun

tīng shuō zhè cì cè shì de nán dù hěn gāo
听说，这次测试的难度很高。
I heard that the **test** this time is very difficult.

71 曾(经)   céng (jīng)   **Adverb:** once; in the past

tā **céng** shì wǒ xīn ài de nǚ yǒu,   xiàn zài zhǐ shì pǔ
她 **曾** 是 我 心 爱 的 女 友 ， 现 在 只 是 普
tōng péng yǒu
通 朋 友 。
She was **once** a beloved girlfriend, now just an ordinary friend.

72 茶叶   chá yè   **Noun:** tea leaves

ōu méng guó jiā cóng zhōng guó jìn kǒu le dà liàng de **chá yè**
欧 盟 国 家 从 中 国 进 口 了 大 量 的 **茶 叶** 。
EU countries import a large amount of **tea leaves** from China.

73 产品   chǎn pǐn   **Noun:** product

zhè xiē **chǎn pǐn** de zhì liàng hěn hǎo,   fēi cháng shòu huān yíng
这 些 **产 品** 的 质 量 很 好 ， 非 常 受 欢 迎 。
These **products** are of good quality and very popular.

74 长途   cháng tú   **Adjective:** long-distance

tā men jīng guò **cháng tú** yùn shū,   yí gè yuè cái dào
它 们 经 过 **长 途** 运 输 ， 一 个 月 才 到
ōu zhōu
欧 洲 。
Through **long-distance** travel, they take a month to reach Europe.

75 常识   cháng shí   **Noun:** common sense

yǒu xiē rén méi yǒu shòu guò jiào yù,   quē fá **cháng shí**
有 些 人 没 有 受 过 教 育 ， 缺 乏 **常 识** 。
Some people are uneducated and lack **common sense**.

76 唱片   chàng piàn   **Noun:** music record; disc

wǒ men dōu shōu jí le liú xíng gē wáng de chàng piàn
我 们 都 收 集 了 流 行 歌 王 的 **唱 片** 。
We all collected the **music records** of the King of Pop.

77 抄   chāo   **Verb:** to copy; to plagiarize

rú guǒ bié rén chāo le nǐ de zuò pǐn kě yǐ jǔ bào
如 果 别 人 **抄** 了 你 的 作 品 ， 可 以 举 报 。
If someone else **copied** your work, you can report it.

78 抄写   chāo xiě   **Verb:** to transcribe; to copy and write down

lǎo shī ràng wǒ chāo xiě cí yǔ hé jù zi
老 师 让 我 **抄 写** 词 语 和 句 子 。
The teacher asked me **to copy and write down** words and sentences.

79 潮   cháo   **Noun:** tide; wave

děng cháo tuì le wǒ men zài yóu yǒng
等 **潮** 退 了 ， 我 们 再 游 泳 。
Wait for the **tide** to go out, then let's swim again.

80 潮流   cháo liú   **Noun:** trend; fashion

tā tōng cháng zài shén me fāng miàn gǎn cháo liú
他 通 常 在 什 么 方 面 赶 **潮 流** ？
In what aspects does he usually follow the **trend**?

81 潮湿   cháo shī   **Adjective:** damp; wet

zhè gè guó jiā de běi biān gān zào nán biān cháo shī
这 个 国 家 的 北 边 干 燥 ， 南 边 **潮 湿** 。
The north of this country is dry and the south is **wet**.

82 彻底 chè dǐ
Adjective: thorough
Adverb: thoroughly; completely

Adj.
wǒ xū yào shí jiān gěi zhè jiàn shì yí gè chè dǐ de sī kǎo
我需要时间给这件事一个**彻底**的思考。
I need time to give this matter a **thorough** thought.

Adv.
wǒ xiǎng chè dǐ wàng jì yǐ qián tòng kǔ de huí yì
我想**彻底**忘记以前痛苦的回忆。
I want to **completely** forget the painful memories of the past.

83 沉 chén
Verb: to sink

zāo gāo wǒ de xiàng liàn chén le wǒ yào qù lāo
糟糕！我的项链**沉**了，我要去捞。
Oops! My necklace **sank**, I'm going to fish it out.

84 沉默 chén mò
Adjective: silent
Noun: silence

Adj.
lǐng dǎo xī wàng yuán gōng duì zhè gè ān pái bǎo chí chén mò
领导希望员工对这个安排保持**沉默**。
The leader wants staff to keep **silent** about this arrangement.

Noun
kě shì chén mò bú dài biǎo fú cóng
可是**沉默**不代表服从。
But **silence** does not mean obedience.

85 沉(重) chén zhòng
Adjective: heavy

zuì jìn gōng zuò yā lì tài chén zhòng wǒ gāi zěn me bàn
最近工作压力太**沉重**，我该怎么办？
The work pressure is too **heavy** recently, what should I do?

86 称赞   chēng zàn   **Verb:** to praise; to compliment
Noun: praise; compliment

Verb
lǎo bǎn zài huì yì shàng chēng zàn le wǒ de gōng zuò néng lì
老 板 在 会 议 上 **称 赞** 了 我 的 工 作 能 力 。
The boss **praised** my work ability in the meeting.

Noun
tā de chēng zàn ràng wǒ fēi cháng gāo xìng
他 的 **称 赞** 让 我 非 常 高 兴 。
His **compliment** made me very happy.

87 成人   chéng rén   **Noun:** adult

xiǎo hái hé chéng rén de sī wéi bù yí yàng
小 孩 和 **成 人** 的 思 维 不 一 样 。
Children and **adults** have different mindsets.

88 诚实   chéng shí   **Adjective:** honest

tā cháng cháng sā huǎng yì diǎn yě bù chéng shí
她 常 常 撒 谎 ， 一 点 也 不 **诚 实** 。
She often lies and is not **honest** at all.

89 诚信   chéng xìn   **Noun:** honesty; integrity

chéng xìn hé tòu míng shì wǒ men de hé zuò yuán zé
诚 信 和 透 明 是 我 们 的 合 作 原 则 。
Integrity and transparency are our principles of cooperation.

90 承担   chéng dān   **Verb:** to bear (responsibility, costs)

fū qī yào yì qǐ chéng dān jiā tíng zé rèn
夫 妻 要 一 起 **承 担** 家 庭 责 任 。
Husband and wife need **to bear** family responsibilities together.

91 承受   chéng shòu   **Verb:** to bear (feelings, pressure); to endure

lí hūn hòu，tā yí gè rén chéng shòu le hěn duō tòng kǔ
离 婚 后，她 一 个 人 **承 受** 了 很 多 痛 苦。
After the divorce, she **bore** a lot of pain alone.

92 承认   chéng rèn   **Verb:** to admit

tā fàn cuò le què bù chéng rèn，shì pà méi miàn zi
他 犯 错 了 却 不 **承 认**，是 怕 没 面 子。
He made mistakes but didn't **admit** it because he feared losing face.

93 程序   chéng xù   **Noun:** App (computer program)

shì zhè gè chéng xù yuán chuàng jiàn le zhè gè chéng xù
是 这 个 程 序 员 创 建 了 这 个 **程 序**。
It was this programmer who created this **app**.

94 吃惊   chī jīng   **Adjective:** shocked; amazed

wǒ hěn chī jīng tā yǒu zhè yàng de cái huá
我 很 **吃 惊** 他 有 这 样 的 才 华！
I'm **amazed** he has such a talent!

95 迟到   chí dào   **Adjective:** late (time)

duì bu qǐ，lù shàng dǔ chē，wǒ huì chí dào shí fēn zhōng
对 不 起，路 上 堵 车，我 会 **迟 到** 十 分 钟。
Sorry, there is traffic jam, I'll be ten minutes **late**.

96 尺   chǐ   **Measurement:** Chinese foot (⅓ meter)

tā de shēn gāo zhǐ yǒu liù chǐ
他 的 身 高 只 有 六 **尺**。
His height is only 6 **feet**.

97 尺寸   chǐ cùn   **Noun:** size; dimension

zhè shuāng xié zi de chǐ cùn tài xiǎo， wǒ yào huàn
这 双 鞋 子 的 **尺 寸** 太 小 ， 我 要 换 。

The **size** of this pair of shoes is too small, I want to exchange.

98 尺子   chǐ zi   **Noun:** ruler

zhè bǎ chǐ zi shì zài yà mǎ xùn shàng mǎi de
这 把 **尺 子** 是 在 亚 马 逊 上 买 的 。

I bought this **ruler** on Amazon.

99 冲   chōng   **Verb:** to rush; to rinse; to flush

hóng shuǐ cóng gāo chù chōng xià lái， yān le zhè tiáo lù
洪 水 从 高 处 **冲** 下 来 ， 淹 了 这 条 路 。

The flood **rushed** down from the heights and flooded the road.

shén me？ tā wàng jì chōng mǎ tǒng le
什 么 ？ 他 忘 记 **冲** 马 桶 了 ？

What? He forgot **to flush** the toilet?

100 充电   chōng diàn   **Verb:** to charge (electricity)

wǒ de shǒu jī méi diàn le， wǒ yào chōng diàn
我 的 手 机 没 电 了 ， 我 要 **充 电** 。

My phone is out of battery, I need **to charge** it.

101 充电器   chōng diàn qì   **Noun:** charger

wǒ de diàn nǎo chōng diàn qì huài le， wǒ děi mǎi xīn de
我 的 电 脑 **充 电 器** 坏 了 ， 我 得 买 新 的 。

My computer **charger** is broken; I have to buy a new one.

102 充分   chōng fèn   **Adjective:** full; ample
Adverb: fully

Adj.
qí shí， fēn shǒu bù xū yào chōng fèn de lǐ yóu
其 实 ， 分 手 不 需 要 **充 分** 的 理 由 。
In fact, breaking up doesn't need a **full** reason.

Adv.
zuì jìn tā zài chōng fèn de zhǔn bèi gōng zuò miàn shì
最 近 她 在 **充 分** 地 准 备 工 作 面 试 。
Recently she is **fully** preparing for work interview.

103 虫子   chóng zi   **Noun:** insect; worm; bug

wǒ kàn dào yì zhī niǎo zài shù shàng chī chóng zi
我 看 到 一 只 鸟 在 树 上 吃 **虫 子** 。
I saw a bird eating **worms** on a tree.

104 抽   chōu   **Verb:** to pump; to take out

tā cóng xìn fēng lǐ chōu chū le yì zhāng kǎ piàn hé
她 从 信 封 里 **抽** 出 了 一 张 卡 片 和
yì bǎi ōu yuán
一 百 欧 元 。
She **took out** a card and 100 euros from the envelope.

105 抽奖   chōu jiǎng   **Verb:** to draw (play) the lottery

wǒ cóng lái bù chōu jiǎng， yīn wèi zhòng jiǎng lǜ tài dī
我 从 来 不 **抽 奖** ， 因 为 中 奖 率 太 低 。
I never **play the lottery** because the odds of winning are too low.

106 抽烟   chōu yān   **Verb:** to smoke

wǒ lǎo gōng hěn hǎo， bù chōu yān， yě bù xù jiǔ
我 老 公 很 好 ， 不 **抽 烟** ， 也 不 酗 酒 。
My husband is good, he neither **smokes** nor drinks heavily.

107 出口   chū kǒu   **Noun:** exit
Verb: to export

Noun

电 影 院 的 入 口 在 前 面，**出 口** 在 后 面。
diàn yǐng yuàn de rù kǒu zài qián miàn chū kǒu zài hòu miàn

The entrance to the cinema is at the front and the **exit** is at the back.

Verb

西 班 牙 向 欧 洲 大 陆 **出 口** 海 鲜。
xī bān yá xiàng ōu zhōu dà lù chū kǒu hǎi xiān

Spain **exports** seafood to continental Europe.

108 出色   chū sè   **Adjective:** excellent; outstanding

我 的 前 男 友 是 一 个 **出 色** 的 推 销 员。
wǒ de qián nán yǒu shì yí gè chū sè de tuī xiāo yuán

My ex-boyfriend was an **excellent** salesman.

109 出售   chū shòu   **Verb:** to sell

他 的 日 常 工 作 是 **出 售** 二 手 车。
tā de rì cháng gōng zuò shì chū shòu èr shǒu chē

His day job was **selling** second-hand cars.

110 出席   chū xí   **Verb:** to attend (formal occasions)

王 子 和 公 主 们 都 **出 席** 了 女 王 的 葬 礼。
wáng zǐ hé gōng zhǔ men dōu chū xí le nǚ wáng de zàng lǐ

Princes and princesses all **attended** the queen's funeral.

111 处于   chǔ yú   **Verb:** to be in (condition)

他 现 在 **处 于** 绝 境，我 们 必 须 帮 他。
tā xiàn zài chǔ yú jué jìng wǒ men bì xū bāng tā

He **is in** a desperate situation now, we must help him.

112a 处   chǔ   **Verb:** to get along; to handle

kě xī wǒ de gǒu hé māo chǔ de bú tài hǎo
可 惜 我 的 狗 和 猫 **处** 得 不 太 好 。
Unfortunately my dog and cat don't **get along** very well.

112b 处   chù   **Noun:** place (small)

zhè yí chù shì gǒu wō nà yí chù shì māo wō
这 一 **处** 是 狗 窝 ， 那 一 **处** 是 猫 窝 。
This **place** is the dog bed, that **place** is the cat bed.

113 穿上   chuān shàng   **Verb:** to put on (clothes)

nǚ rén chuān shàng xīn niáng zhuāng dōu tè bié měi
女 人 **穿 上** 新 娘 装 都 特 别 美 ！
Women are all so beautiful in (once **put on**) bridal attire!

114 传统   chuán tǒng   **Noun:** tradition
                                      Adjective: traditional

Noun
měi gè guó jiā dōu yǒu zì jǐ de chuán tǒng hé wén huà
每 个 国 家 都 有 自 己 的 **传 统** 和 文 化 。
Every country has its own **traditions** and culture.

Adj.
zhōng guó chuán tǒng de xīn niáng zhuāng hé xīn láng zhuāng dōu shì
中 国 **传 统** 的 新 娘 装 和 新 郎 装 都 是
hóng sè
红 色 。
Chinese **traditional** bridal and groomal attire are both red.

115 窗户   chuāng hu   **Noun:** window

wǒ yào xuǎn hé wǒ de chuāng hu dā pèi de chuāng lián
我 要 选 和 我 的 **窗 户** 搭 配 的 窗 帘 。
I want to choose curtains that can match my **windows**.

116 窗子　　chuāng zi　　**Noun:** window

下暴风雨了，快去关窗子。
xià bào fēng yǔ le, kuài qù guān chuāng zi

It's storming, quickly go to close the **windows**

117 窗台　　chuāng tái　　**Noun:** windowsill

在周末，我喜欢坐在窗台看书。
zài zhōu mò, wǒ xǐ huān zuò zài chuāng tái kàn shū

On weekends, I like to sit on the **windowsill** and read books.

118 春季　　chūn jì　　**Noun:** springtime

春季是我最喜欢的季节，你呢？
chūn jì shì wǒ zuì xǐ huān de jì jié, nǐ ne

Springtime is my favorite season, how about you?

119 纯　　chún　　**Adjective:** pure

我的孩子们不喜欢喝纯牛奶。
wǒ de hái zi men bù xǐ huān hē chún niú nǎi

My kids don't like drinking **pure** milk.

120 纯净水　　chún jìng shuǐ　　**Noun:** purified water

我要去给伙伴们买几瓶纯净水。
wǒ yào qù gěi huǒ bàn men mǎi jǐ píng chún jìng shuǐ

I'm going to buy several bottles of **purified water** for my mates.

121 词汇　　cí huì　　**Noun:** vocabulary

这本书大概包含了一千个词汇。
zhè běn shū dà gài bāo hán le yì qiān gè cí huì

This book contains about a thousand **vocabulary**.

122 此   cǐ   **Pronoun:** this; here (formal)

^{qíng} ^{bào} ^{jú} ^{huái} ^{yí} ^{cǐ} ^{rén} ^{shì} ^{jiàn} ^{dié}
情 报 局 怀 疑 **此** 人 是 间 谍。
The intelligence agency suspects that **this** person is a spy.

123 此外   cǐ wài   **Conjunction:** in addition; moreover

^{cǐ} ^{wài}   ^{tā} ^{yǒu} ^{duō} ^{guó} ^{de} ^{guó} ^{jí}   ^{bù} ^{róng} ^{yì} ^{duì} ^{fu}
此 外，他 有 多 国 的 国 籍，不 容 易 对 付。
Moreover, he has many nationalities and is not easy to deal with.

124 次   cì   **Adverb:** secondary (use with other words) **Noun:** time (sequence)

Adv.
^{bǎo} ^{chí} ^{jiàn} ^{kāng} ^{shì} ^{zuì} ^{zhòng} ^{yào} ^{de} ^{zhèng} ^{qián} ^{shì} ^{cì} ^{yào} ^{de}
保 持 健 康 是 最 重 要 的, 挣 钱 是 **次 要** 的。
Staying healthy is the most important, earning money is **secondary**.

Noun
^{dù} ^{jià} ^{de} ^{shí} ^{hou}   ^{wǒ} ^{zuò} ^{guò} ^{liǎng} ^{cì} ^{àn} ^{mó}
度 假 的 时 候 ， 我 做 过 两 **次** 按 摩。
While on vacation, I had a massage twice (two **times**).

125 刺   cì   **Noun:** thorn

^{xiǎo} ^{xīn}   ^{méi} ^{guī} ^{huā} ^{shàng} ^{yǒu} ^{hěn} ^{duō} ^{cì}
小 心 ！ 玫 瑰 花 上 有 很 多 **刺** 。
Be careful! There are many **thorns** on the rose.

126 刺激   cì jī   **Verb:** to stimulate

^{zhè} ^{bù} ^{diàn} ^{yǐng} ^{cì} ^{jī} ^{dào} ^{le} ^{tā} ^{tòng} ^{kǔ} ^{de} ^{jì} ^{yì}
这 部 电 影 **刺 激** 到 了 他 痛 苦 的 记 忆。
The film **stimulated** his painful memory.

127 从此　　　cóng cǐ　　**Adverb:** henceforth; from this point on; since then

cóng cǐ　　tā chángcháng zuò è mèng
从 此 ， 他 常 常 做 噩 梦 。
Since then, he often has nightmares.

128 粗　　　cū　　**Adjective:** thick; rough

zhè zhī gāng bǐ tài cū ， wǒ yào xì de
这 支 钢 笔 太 粗 ， 我 要 细 的 。
This pen is too **thick**, I want a fine (thin) one.

129 粗心　　　cū xīn　　**Adjective:** careless

zuò bào gào de shí hou ， tā yǒu shí hou hěn cū xīn
做 报 告 的 时 候 ， 她 有 时 候 很 粗 心 。
When doing reports, she is sometimes **careless**.

130 促进　　　cù jìn　　**Verb:** to boost; to advance

zǒng tǒng de fǎng wèn cù jìn le liǎng gè guó jiā de guān xi
总 统 的 访 问 促 进 了 两 个 国 家 的 关 系 。
The president's visit **boosted** relations between the two countries.

131 促使　　　cù shǐ　　**Verb:** to impel; to urge; to prompt

zhè cì bǐ sài cù shǐ dà jiā xiāng hù jìng zhēng
这 次 比 赛 促 使 大 家 相 互 竞 争 。
This competition **impels** everyone to compete against each other.

132 促销 cù xiāo
Verb: to promote (sales)
Noun: promotion

Verb
zhè wèi wǎng hóng zài píng tái shàng cù xiāo hóng jiǔ
这 位 网 红 在 平 台 上 **促 销** 红 酒 。
The influencer is **promoting** red wine on the platform.

Noun
zài tā de cù xiāo xià xiāo liàng yǐ jīng dào le shí wàn píng
在 他 的 **促 销** 下 ， 销 量 已 经 到 了 十 万 瓶 。
Under his **promotion**, sales have reached 100,000 bottles.

133 措施 cuò shī
Noun: measure

kàn lái gōng sī de shì chǎng cuò shī hěn yǒu xiào
看 来 ， 公 司 的 市 场 **措 施** 很 有 效 。
It appears that the company's marketing **measure** is effective.

134 打 dǎ
Verb: to strike; to hit; to beat

nà gè hún dàn jiā bào zǒng shì dǎ rén
那 个 混 蛋 家 暴 ， 总 是 **打** 人 。
That jerk is domestically violent and **beats** people all the time.

135 答案 dá àn
Noun: answer

zhè gè wèn tí zhēn de zhǐ yǒu yí gè dá àn ma
这 个 问 题 真 的 只 有 一 个 **答 案** 吗 ？
Is there really only one **answer** to this question?

136 打败 dǎ bài
Verb: to defeat; to beat

hā ha dà pàng zi xuǎn shǒu zhōng yú bèi dǎ bài le
哈 哈 ！ 大 胖 子 选 手 终 于 被 **打 败** 了 。
Ha ha! The big fat contestant is finally **defeated**.

137 打雷　　　　dǎ léi　　　**Verb:** thunder

zuó wǎn yòu dǎ léi yòu shǎn diàn　wǒ fēi cháng hài pà
昨 晚 又 **打 雷** 又 闪 电， 我 非 常 害 怕。
It was **thundering** with lightning last night, I was very scared.

138 打扫　　　　dǎ sǎo　　　**Verb:** to clean (places)

wǒ de qīng jié gōng měi zhōu liù lái dǎ sǎo wǒ de gōng yù
我 的 清 洁 工 每 周 六 来 **打 扫** 我 的 公 寓。
My cleaner comes **to clean** my apartment every Saturday.

139 打折　　　　dǎ zhé　　　**Verb:** to discount

fú zhuāng diàn zhè jǐ tiān zài dǎ zhé　wǒ bù néng cuò guò
服 装 店 这 几 天 在 **打 折**， 我 不 能 错 过。
The clothing store is **discounting** these days, I can't miss it.

140 打针　　　　dǎ zhēn　　　**Verb:** to get/give an injection

wǒ ér zi pà dǎ zhēn　wǒ bì xū gǔ lì tā
我 儿 子 怕 **打 针**， 我 必 须 鼓 励 他。
My son is afraid of **getting injections**, I have to encourage him.

141 大巴　　　　dà bā　　　**Noun:** coach

zhè liàng dà bā de sī jī shì wǒ de lín jū
这 辆 **大 巴** 的 司 机 是 我 的 邻 居。
The driver of this **coach** is my neighbor.

142 大多　　　　dà duō　　　**Adverb:** mostly; for the most part

tā de dà bā dà duō zài nán jīng hé shàng hǎi wǎng fǎn
他 的 大 巴 **大 多** 在 南 京 和 上 海 往 返。
His coach **mostly** go back and forth between Nanjing and Shanghai.

143 大方　dà fang　**Adjective:** generous

tā yǐ qián hěn xiǎo qì,　xiàn zài hěn dà fang
他 以 前 很 小 气，现 在 很 **大 方**。
He used to be very stingy, but now he is very **generous**.

144 大哥　dà gē　**Noun:** big brother; eldest brother

nǐ kàn,　nà gè qiáng zhuàng de nán de shì wǒ dà gē
你 看，那 个 强 壮 的 男 的 是 我 **大 哥**。
You see, that strong man is my **eldest brother**.

145 大规模　dà guī mó　**Adjective:** extensive large-scale

zāo gāo! dí guó zhèng zài jìn xíng dà guī mó de jìn gōng
糟 糕！敌 国 正 在 进 行 **大 规 模** 的 进 攻。
Terrible! The enemy country is launching on a **large-scale** attack.

146 大会　dà huì　**Noun:** general meeting; general assembly

zhè gè dà huì guī dìng měi gè rén dōu yào cān jiā
这 个 **大 会** 规 定 每 个 人 都 要 参 加。
This **general meeting** requires everyone to participate.

147 大姐　dà jiě　**Noun:** big sister; eldest sister

wǒ de dà jiě shēng zhí zuò le bù mén zhǔ guǎn
我 的 **大 姐** 升 职 做 了 部 门 主 管。
My **eldest sister** has been promoted to be department head.

148 大楼　dà lóu　**Noun:** building; large building

zhè jiā fáng dì chǎn gōng sī gòu mǎi le hěn duō dà lóu
这 家 房 地 产 公 司 购 买 了 很 多 **大 楼**。
This real estate company bought many **large buildings**.

149 大陆　dà lù　**Noun:** continent; mainland China

xiāng gǎng rén cháng cháng qù dà lù tàn qīn
香 港 人 常 常 去 **大 陆** 探 亲。
Hong Kong people often go to the **mainland (China)** to visit relatives.

150 大妈　dà mā　**Noun:** aunt; older woman (negative term)

wǒ dà mā jīn nián wǔ shí duō suì le hái méi tuì xiū
我 **大 妈** 今 年 五 十 多 岁 了， 还 没 退 休。
My **aunt** is in her fifties this year and hasn't retired yet.

wǒ de tóng shì hěn shēng qì yīn wèi yǒu rén shuō tā shì
我 的 同 事 很 生 气， 因 为 有 人 说 她 是
dà mā
大 妈！
My colleague is angry because someone said she is an **older woman**!

151 大型　dà xíng　**Adjective:** large (vehicles)

xiǎo xíng chē zhōng xíng chē hé dà xíng chē wǒ men gōng
小 型 车， 中 型 车 和 **大 型** 车， 我 们 公
sī dōu shēng chǎn
司 都 生 产。
Small cars, medium cars and **large** cars, our company produces all.

152 大爷　dà ye　**Noun:** respectful term to address an old man

tīng shuō nà wèi dà ye shì tuì yì lǎo bīng
听 说 那 位 **大 爷** 是 退 役 老 兵。
I heard that **old gentleman** is a retired veteran.

153 大众　dà zhòng　**Noun:** public; the mass

nǐ guān zhù nǎ xiē dà zhòng méi tǐ
你 关 注 哪 些 **大 众** 媒 体？
Which **mass** media do you follow?

154 代替   dài tì   **Verb:** to replace (roles)

他 辞 职 了 ， 我 得 找 新 员 工 代 替 他 的
tā cí zhí le   wǒ děi zhǎo xīn yuán gōng dài tì tā de

职 位 。
zhí wèi

He resigned and I had to find a new employee **to replace** his role.

155 待遇   dài yù   **Noun:** treatment

其 实 ， 公 司 的 奖 金 待 遇 还 不 错 。
qí shí   gōng sī de jiǎng jīn dài yù hái bú cuò

In fact, the company's bonus **treatment** is not bad.

156 袋   dài   **Noun:** bag; sack; pouch

我 去 中 国 超 市 买 了 一 大 袋 米 。
wǒ qù zhōng guó chāo shì mǎi le yí dà dài mǐ

I went to the Chinese supermarket to buy a big **bag** of rice.

157 戴   dài   **Verb:** to wear (accessories)

我 不 喜 欢 戴 手 链 ， 但 喜 欢 戴 手 表 。
wǒ bù xǐ huān dài shǒu liàn   dàn xǐ huān dài shǒu biǎo

I don't like **wearing** bracelets, but I like **wearing** watches.

158 担保   dān bǎo   **Verb:** to guarantee; to assure; to ensure

我 弟 向 我 担 保 以 后 不 再 吸 毒 。
wǒ dì xiàng wǒ dān bǎo yǐ hòu bù zài xī dú

My brother **assured** me that he would never take drugs again.

159 担任   dān rèn   **Verb:** to serve as (jobs)

zǒng cái xī wàng wáng xiān shēng dān rèn tā de fù zǒng cái
总 裁 希 望 王 先 生 **担 任** 他 的 副 总 裁 。
The CEO wants Mr. Wang **to serve as** his deputy CEO.

160 担心   dān xīn   **Verb:** to worry
Adjective: worried

Verb

bié dān xīn tā de shāng bù yán zhòng
别 **担 心** ， 她 的 伤 不 严 重 。
Don't **worry**, her injuries are not severe.

Adj.

kě shì wǒ dān xīn zhì liáo fèi yòng tài gāo
可 是 我 **担 心** 治 疗 费 用 太 高 。
However, I'm **worried** the cost of treatment is too high.

161 单   dān   **Adjective:** single (use with other words); odd (number)

tā dān shēn wǔ nián le zài kǎo lǜ xiāng qīn
她 **单 身** 五 年 了 ， 在 考 虑 相 亲 。
She's been **single** for 5 years and is considering a blind date.

zhè dòng lóu de fáng hào zhǐ yǒu shuāng shù méi yǒu dān shù
这 栋 楼 的 房 号 只 有 双 数 ， 没 有 **单 数** 。
The apartment numbers of this building only have even numbers, no **odd** numbers.

162 单纯   dān chún   **Adjective:** pure; simple (people)

dà xué shēng méi yǒu shè huì jīng yàn sī xiǎng dān chún
大 学 生 没 有 社 会 经 验 ， 思 想 **单 纯** 。
University students have no social experience and their thinking is **simple**.

163 单调   dān diào   **Adjective:** boring; monotonous

wǒ rèn wéi xíng zhèng gōng zuò yǒu diǎn dān diào
我 认 为 行 政 工 作 有 点 **单 调** 。
I find administrative work a bit **boring**.

164 单独   dān dú   **Adverb:** alone

wǒ kě yǐ gēn nǐ dān dú tán yi tán ma
我 可 以 跟 你 **单 独** 谈 一 谈 吗 ？
Can I have a chat with you **alone**?

165 淡   dàn   **Adjective:** light; weak (color or flavor)

zhè dào cài de wèi dào tài dàn le bù gòu nóng
这 道 菜 的 味 道 太 **淡** 了 ， 不 够 浓 ！
The flavor of this dish is too **weak**, not strong enough!

166 导游   dǎo yóu   **Noun:** tour guide

zhè wèi dǎo yóu jiǎng jiě de fēi cháng hǎo
这 位 **导 游** 讲 解 得 非 常 好 ！
The **tour guide** explained it very well!

167 导致   dǎo zhì   **Verb:** to cause (negative)

quán qiú nuǎn huà dǎo zhì le hěn duō bīng chuān róng huà
全 球 暖 化 **导 致** 了 很 多 冰 川 融 化 。
Global warming has **caused** many glaciers to melt.

168 倒闭   dǎo bì   **Verb:** to close down

yóu yú wǎng gòu tài huǒ hěn duō shí tǐ diàn dǎo bì le
由 于 网 购 太 火 ， 很 多 实 体 店 **倒 闭** 了 。
Due to the popularity of online shopping, many physical stores **closed down**.

169a 倒车

dǎo chē

Verb: to change trains or buses

wǒ men kě yǐ zài nà biān de zhàn tái dǎo chē
我 们 可 以 在 那 边 的 站 台 **倒 车** 。
We can **change trains** on the platform over there.

169b 倒车

dào chē

Verb: to reverse (cars)

wǒ yào dào chē qǐng nǐ men hòu tuì
我 要 **倒 车** ， 请 你 们 后 退 。
I need to **reverse the car**, please step back.

170 得意

dé yì

Adjective: proud (negative or sarcastic)

tā zuì jìn shēng zhí chéng zǒng jiān le fēi cháng dé yì
他 最 近 升 职 成 总 监 了 ， 非 常 **得 意** ！
He was recently promoted to be a director, very **proud**!

171 得罪

dé zuì

Verb: to offend

tā shì lǎo bǎn de biǎo gē suǒ yǐ méi rén gǎn dé zuì tā
他 是 老 板 的 表 哥 ，所 以 没 人 敢 **得 罪** 他 。
He is the cousin of the boss, so no one dares **to offend** him.

172 得

děi

Verb: to need; must

zhè zhǎn dēng huài le wǒ men děi huàn dēng pào
这 盏 灯 坏 了 ， 我 们 **得** 换 灯 泡 。
This lamp is broken, we **must** change the bulb.

173 灯光

dēng guāng

Noun: stage lighting; light/lighting (artifical)

wǒ yào mǎi kě yǐ tiáo jié dēng guāng de dēng pào
我 要 买 可 以 调 节 **灯 光** 的 灯 泡 。
I want to buy light bulbs with adjustable **lighting**.

174 登　　dēng　　**Verb:** to ascend; to mount

zhè dòng lóu nà me gāo, tā shì zěn me dēng shàng qù de
这栋楼那么高，他是怎么**登**上去的？
The building is so tall, how did he **ascend** it?

175 登记　　dēng jì　　**Verb:** to register; to check-in

wǒ men xiān qù qián tái dēng jì, zài qù chī fàn
我们先去前台**登记**，再去吃饭。
Let's go to the front desk **to register** first, and then go to eat.

176 登录　　dēng lù　　**Verb:** to sign in; to log in

méi yǒu mì mǎ, jiù bù néng dēng lù zhè tái diàn nǎo
没有密码，就不能**登录**这台电脑。
Without the password, you cannot **log in** to this computer.

177 登山　　dēng shān　　**Verb:** to do mountain-climbing

wǒ cóng xiǎo jiù xǐ huān huá xuě hé dēng shān
我从小就喜欢滑雪和**登山**。
I have loved skiing and **mountain climbing** since I was a child.

178 的确　　dí què　　**Adverb:** indeed; certainly

kàn lái, nǐ dí què shì gè ài mào xiǎn de rén
看来，你**的确**是个爱冒险的人。
It seems that you are **certainly** an adventurous person.

179 敌人　　dí rén　　**Noun:** enemy

wǒ hé tā yǐ qián shì dí rén, xiàn zài shì péng yǒu
我和他以前是**敌人**，现在是朋友。
He and I used to be **enemies**, but now we are friends.

180 底　　dǐ　　**Noun:** bottom; end

tā cóng lái dōu bù gǎn chù pèng wǒ de dǐ xiàn
他 从 来 都 不 敢 触 碰 我 的 **底** 线 ！
He never dared to touch my **bottom** line!

181 地方　　dì fang　　**Noun:** place

zhè gè dì fang shì dāng dì yǒu míng de shāng wù yuán
这 个 **地 方** 是 当 地 有 名 的 商 务 园 。
This **place** is a well-known local business park.

182 地面　　dì miàn　　**Noun:** ground; floor; surface

wǒ xiǎng zài jiā lǐ ān zhuāng mù bǎn dì miàn
我 想 在 家 里 安 装 木 板 **地 面** 。
I want to install wooden **floor** in my home.

183 地位　　dì wèi　　**Noun:** status

duì yú lǎo bǎn dì wèi hé míng shēng tóng yàng zhòng yào
对 于 老 板 ， **地 位** 和 名 声 同 样 重 要 ！
For the boss, **status** and reputation are equally important!

184 地下　　dì xià　　**Noun:** underground

tā hěn qióng zhù zài yí gè dì xià shì
他 很 穷 ， 住 在 一 个 **地 下** 室 。
He is very poor and lives in a basement (**underground** room).

185 地址　　dì zhǐ　　**Noun:** address

tā shén zhì bù hǎo yì si gào sù bié rén zì jǐ de dì zhǐ
他 甚 至 不 好 意 思 告 诉 别 人 自 己 的 **地 址** 。
He's even embarrassed to tell other people his own **address**.

186 典型　diǎn xíng　**Adjective:** typical

zhè guǒ rán shì diǎn xíng de qióng rén　zhēn kě lián
这 果 然 是 **典 型** 的 穷 人 ！真 可 怜 ！
This is indeed a **typical** poor person! So pitiful!

187 点名　diǎn míng　**Verb:** take rollcall; to mention sb. by name

tīng shuō zài kǎo shì zhī qián　lǎo shī yào diǎn míng
听 说 在 考 试 之 前 ，老 师 要 **点 名** 。
I heard that before the exam, the teacher will **take rollcall**.

188 电灯　diàn dēng　**Noun:** electric light; electric lamp

zhè jiā gōng sī shì wǒ men de diàn dēng gōng yìng shāng
这 家 公 司 是 我 们 的 **电 灯** 供 应 商 。
This company is our **electric lighting** supplier.

189 电动车　diàn dòng chē　**Noun:** electric car

tā men yě xiāo shòu diàn dòng chē　zhì liàng fēi cháng hǎo
他 们 也 销 售 **电 动 车** ，质 量 非 常 好 ！
They also sell **electric cars** and the quality is very good!

190 电梯　diàn tī　**Noun:** elevator

wǒ de gōng yù zài　lóu děi zuò diàn tī shàng qù
我 的 公 寓 在 15 楼 ，得 坐 **电 梯** 上 去 。
My apartment is on the 15th floor, I need to take the **elevator** up.

191 电源　diàn yuán　**Noun:** power supply

zāo gāo　diàn yuán bèi qiē duàn le　zěn me bàn
糟 糕 ！**电 源** 被 切 断 了 ！怎 么 办 ？
Oops! The **power supply** has been cut off! What to do?

192 顶　　　　　　　dǐng

Noun: top
(use with other words)

fàng xīn　yǒu rén gāng gāng qù lóu dǐng chá kàn le
放 心，有 人 刚 刚 去 楼 顶 查 看 了。
Don't worry, someone just went to the **rooftop** to check.

193 定　　　　　　　dìng

Verb: to settle;
to decide
(use with other words)

zhè jiàn shì hái méi dìng　yīn wèi zǒng jīng lǐ hái méi jué dìng
这 件 事 还 没 定！因 为 总 经 理 还 没 决 定。
This matter is still un**settled**! Because the CEO has not yet **decided**.

194 冬季　　　　　　dōng jì　　**Noun:** winter

wǒ zhí zi shēng zài qiū jì　zhí nǚ shēng zài dōng jì
我 侄 子 生 在 秋 季，侄 女 生 在 冬 季。
My nephew was born in autumn, my niece was born in **winter**.

195 动画片　　　　　dòng huà piàn　　**Noun:** cartoon movies

tā men měi tiān wǎn shàng diǎn zhǔn shí kàn dòng huà piàn
他 们 每 天 晚 上8点 准 时 看 动 画 片。
They watch **cartoons** at 8 o'clock on the dot every night.

196 动摇　　　　　　dòng yáo

Verb: to shake;
to waver

rèn hé shì dōu bù huì dòng yáo wǒ de jué xīn
任 何 事 都 不 会 动 摇 我 的 决 心！
Nothing will **shake** my resolve!

197 豆腐　　　　　　dòu fu　　**Noun:** tofu

hěn duō wài guó rén bù xǐ huān chī chòu dòu fu
很 多 外 国 人 不 喜 欢 吃 臭 豆 腐。
Many foreigners don't like to eat stinky **tofu**.

198 独立　　　dú lì　　　**Adjective:** independent

wǒ fēi cháng xīn shǎng tā dú lì de xìng gé
我 非 常 欣 赏 他 **独 立** 的 性 格 。
I really appreciate his **independent** character.

199 独特　　　dú tè　　　**Adjective:** unique; distinctive

tā de shì pín fēi cháng dú tè chōng mǎn chuàng yì
他 的 视 频 非 常 **独 特** ， 充 满 创 意 ！
His videos are very **unique** and full of creativity!

200 独自　　　dú zì　　　**Adverb:** alone; by oneself; one's own

lí hūn hòu tā dú zì fǔ yǎng le liǎng gè hái zi
离 婚 后 ， 她 **独 自** 抚 养 了 两 个 孩 子 。
After the divorce, she raised her two children **alone**.

201 堵　　　dǔ　　　**Verb:** to block **Adjective:** crowded/busy (traffic)

Verb
zhēn dǎo méi mǎ tǒng hǎo xiàng bèi dǔ le
真 倒 霉 ！ 马 桶 好 像 被 **堵** 了 ！
So unlucky! The toilet seems to be **blocked**!

Adj.
jiāo tōng tài dǔ wǒ men kǒng pà huì chí dào
交 通 太 **堵** ， 我 们 恐 怕 会 迟 到 。
The traffic is too **busy**, I'm afraid that we might be late.

202 堵车　　　dǔ chē　　　**Verb:** to cause a traffic jam

qián miàn chū chē huò le suǒ yǐ dǔ chē
前 面 出 车 祸 了 ， 所 以 **堵 车** 。
There was a car accident ahead, so it **caused a traffic jam**.

203 肚子   dù zi   **Noun:** belly; stomach

tā dù zi téng, gāng gāng chōng jìn le cè suǒ
他 **肚子** 疼，刚 刚 冲 进 了 厕 所。
He had a **stomach**ache and just rushed to the toilet.

204 度过   dù guò   **Verb:** to spend time

wǒ xiǎng zhī dào nǐ shì zěn me dù guò dà xué de
我 想 知 道 你 是 怎 么 **度过** 大 学 的？
I would like to know how did you **spend time** in university?

205 锻炼   duàn liàn   **Verb:** to exercise

tā měi tiān zǎo shàng qí zì xíng chē duàn liàn shēn tǐ
他 每 天 早 上 骑 自 行 车 **锻 炼** 身 体。
He **exercises** his body by cycling every morning.

206 对比   duì bǐ   **Verb:** to compare
     Noun: comparison

Verb
gēn tā duì bǐ, wǒ bú gòu qiáng zhuàng
跟 他 **对 比**，我 不 够 强 壮。
Compared to him, I am not strong enough.

Noun
wǒ jué de zhè zhǒng duì bǐ méi yǒu yì yì
我 觉 得 这 种 **对 比** 没 有 意 义。
I find this **comparison** meaningless.

207 对付   duì fu   **Verb:** to deal with

tā zài sī kǎo yīng gāi zěn yàng duì fu tā de zhèng dí
他 在 思 考 应 该 怎 样 **对 付** 他 的 政 敌。
He is pondering how **to deal with** his political opponents.

208 对于   duì yú   **Preposition:** about; regarding

duì yú xīn de dà xuǎn tā hái méi yǒu zhǔn bèi hǎo
对 于 新 的 大 选 ， 他 还 没 有 准 备 好 。
Regarding the new general election, he is still not prepared.

209 多次   duō cì   **Adverb:** repeatedly; many times

tā duō cì shuō ài wǒ kě shì wǒ jiù shì bù xiāng xìn
他 多 次 说 爱 我 ， 可 是 我 就 是 不 相 信 。
He's said **many times** that he loves me, but I just don't believe it.

210 多年   duō nián   **Noun:** many years

zhè me duō nián wǒ měi cì xū yào bāng zhù tā dōu
这 么 多 年 ， 我 每 次 需 要 帮 助 ， 他 都
bù guǎn
不 管 。
For so **many years**, every time I needed help, he never cared.

211 多样   duō yàng   **Adjective:** diverse

xī fāng hūn shā yǒu duō yàng de shè jì hé fēng gé
西 方 婚 纱 有 多 样 的 设 计 和 风 格 。
Western wedding dress have **diverse** designs and styles.

212 多种   duō zhǒng   **Adjective:** multiple; various

lún dūn de táng rén jiē yǒu duō zhǒng zhōng guó měi shí
伦 敦 的 唐 人 街 有 多 种 中 国 美 食 。
London's Chinatown has **various** Chinese delicacies.

213 恶心　　ě xin　　**Adjective:** disgusted; disgusting

tā měi cì shuō zāng huà　wǒ dōu jué de hěn ě xin
他 每 次 说 脏 话 ， 我 都 觉 得 很 **恶 心** 。
Every time he swears, I always find it **disgusting**.

214 儿童　　ér tóng　　**Noun:** children (oppose to adults)

dòng wù yuán duì ér tóng miǎn piào　dàn shì chéng rén yào mǎi piào
动 物 园 对 **儿 童** 免 票 ， 但 是 成 人 要 买 票 。
The zoo is free for **children**, but adults need to buy tickets.

215 而　　ér　　**Conjunction:** yet; and; while

dāng guó jiā de lǐng dǎo shì guāng róng ér kùn nán de
当 国 家 的 领 导 是 光 荣 **而** 困 难 的 。
Being the leader of a country is honorable **yet** difficult.

wǒ xiǎng lí hūn　ér tā zhǐ xiǎng fēn jū
我 想 离 婚 ， **而** 他 只 想 分 居 。
I want a divorce **while** he just wants a separation.

216 而是　　ér shì　　**Conjunction:** but

tā bú shì rì běn rén　ér shì zhōng guó rén
他 不 是 日 本 人 ， **而 是** 中 国 人 。
He is not Japanese, **but** Chinese.

217 耳机　　ěr jī　　**Noun:** headphone; headset

tài bàng le　zhè duì xīn ěr jī yǒu lán yá gōng néng
太 棒 了 ！ 这 对 新 **耳 机** 有 蓝 牙 功 能 。
Great! This new pair of **headphones** has Bluetooth functionality.

218 二手 èr shǒu **Adjective:** second-hand

tā mài le èr shǒu chē hòu cái qù mǎi xīn chē
他 卖 了 **二 手** 车 后 才 去 买 新 车 。
He sold his **second-hand** car before buying a new one.

219 发挥 fā huī **Verb:** to exert; to display; to bring into play

tā xū yào yí fèn hǎo gōng zuò fā huī tā de cái huá
他 需 要 一 份 好 工 作 **发 挥** 他 的 才 华 。
He needs a good job **to display** his talent.

220 发票 fā piào **Noun:** invoice; receipt

qǐng nǐ bǎ diàn zǐ fā piào tōng guò yóu jiàn fā gěi wǒ
请 你 把 电 子 **发 票** 通 过 邮 件 发 给 我 。
Please send me the electronic **invoice** by email.

221 发烧 fā shāo **Verb:** to have a fever

hái zi zài fā shāo kuài qù ná tuì shāo yào
孩 子 在 **发 烧**, 快 去 拿 退 烧 药 。
The child is **having a fever**, go to get antipyretics quickly.

222 法 fǎ **Noun:** way; method

zhè jiàn shì hěn fù zá méi fǎ shuō qīng chǔ
这 件 事 很 复 杂, 没 **法** 说 清 楚 !
This matter is very complicated, there is no **way** to explain clearly!

223 法官 fǎ guān **Noun:** judge (of a court)

zhè wèi fǎ guān kàn shàng qù hěn yán sù
这 位 **法 官** 看 上 去 很 严 肃 !
This **judge** looks very serious!

224 法律

fǎ lǜ

Noun: law; legal

guān yú wéi fǎ dú pǐn, zhōng guó de fǎ lǜ chéng fá hěn yán gé
关于 违 法 毒 品，中 国 的 **法律** 惩 罚 很 严 格。
Regarding illegal drugs, China's **legal** punishment is very strict.

225 法院

fǎ yuàn

Noun: court

tīng shuō qián qī bǎ tā gào shàng le fǎ yuàn
听 说 前 妻 把 他 告 上 了 **法 院**。
I heard that his ex-wife has taken him to **court**.

226 翻

fān

Verb: to turn over

tā gāng gāng tū rán fā huǒ, tī fān le yǐ zi
他 刚 刚 突 然 发 火，踢 **翻** 了 椅 子。
He just lost his temper and kicked **over** the chair.

227 翻译

fān yì

Verb: to translate
Noun: translation

Verb
qǐng bǎ zhè duàn yīng yǔ fān yì chéng zhōng wén
请 把 这 段 英 语 **翻 译** 成 中 文。
Please **translate** this paragraph of English text into Chinese.

Noun
nǐ de fān yì jì qiǎo fēi cháng bàng
你 的 **翻 译** 技 巧 非 常 棒！
Your **translation** skills are fantastic!

228 烦

fán

Verb: to bother
Adjective: annoyed; annoying

Verb
tā zài kāi huì, wǒ men bú yào qù fán tā
他 在 开 会，我 们 不 要 去 **烦** 他。
He's in a meeting, let's not **bother** him.

Adj.
tā kāi huì kāi le yì zhěng tiān, jué de hěn fán
他 开 会 开 了 一 整 天，觉 得 很 **烦**！
He's been in a meeting all day and is feeling **annoyed**!

229 反   fǎn

Verb: to rebel; to reverse
Adjective: inside out

Verb

qí shí, xiǎo hái zi fǎn fù mǔ hěn zhèng cháng
其 实 ， 小 孩 子 **反** 父 母 很 正 常 。
In fact, it is normal for children **to rebel** against parents.

Adj.

zāo gāo ！ wǒ bǎ chèn shān chuān fǎn le ！
糟 糕 ！ 我 把 衬 衫 穿 **反** 了 ！
Oops! I am wearing my shirt **inside out**!

---

230 反而   fǎn ér

Conjunction: instead/ on the contrary

wǒ pī píng tā de shí hou ， tā méi yǒu shēng qì ， fǎn ér
我 批 评 他 的 时 候 ， 他 没 有 生 气 ， **反 而**
xiào le 。
笑 了 。
When I was criticizing him, he was not angry, **instead** he laughed.

---

231 反映   fǎn yìng

Verb: to reflect; to indicate

zhè fǎn yìng le tā gēn běn bù zài hu nǐ de pī píng
这 **反 映** 了 他 根 本 不 在 乎 你 的 批 评 ！
It **reflects** that he didn't care about your criticism at all!

---

232 方   fāng

Adjective: square

yuè bǐng yǒu fāng de ， yě yǒu yuán de
月 饼 有 **方** 的 ， 也 有 圆 的 。
The mooncakes have **square** ones, as well as round ones.

---

233 方案   fāng àn

Noun: plan; scheme; proposal

wǒ fù zé xiě zhè gè xiàng mù de fāng àn
我 负 责 写 这 个 项 目 的 **方 案** 。
I am responsible for writing the **plan** for this project.

234 方针   fāng zhēn   **Noun:** policy; guiding principle

gōng sī huì cóng xià gè yuè kāi shǐ shí shī zhè gè fāng zhēn
公 司 会 从 下 个 月 开 始 实 施 这 个 **方 针**。
The company will start implementing this **policy** next month.

235 放松   fàng sōng   **Verb:** to relax
Adjective: relaxing

Verb
rú guǒ nǐ yā lì tài dà, jiù chū qù fàng sōng yí xià
如 果 你 压 力 太 大 ， 就 出 去 **放 松** 一 下 。
If you're stressed out, go out **to relax** a bit.

Adj.
yì biān sàn bù， yì biān tīng yīn yuè hěn fàng sōng
一 边 散 步 ， 一 边 听 音 乐 很 **放 松**。
Listening to music while walking is very **relaxing**.

236 非   fēi   **Noun:** wrong
(use with other words)

bú yào suí biàn píng jià bié rén de shì fēi
不 要 随 便 评 价 别 人 的 是 **非**。
Don't judge other people's **right and wrong** randomly.

237 肥   féi   **Adjective:** obese; fat;
fertile

yī shēng shuō tā de shēn tǐ tài féi， xū yào jiǎn féi
医 生 说 他 的 身 体 太 **肥** ， 需 要 减 **肥**。
The doctor said his body is too **fat** and needs to lose weight.

238 分布   fēn bù   **Verb:** to distribute
(location); to position
Noun: distribution

Verb
wǒ men de fēn gōng sī fēn bù zài shì jiè gè dì
我 们 的 分 公 司 **分 布** 在 世 界 各 地 。
Our branch companies are **positioned** all over the world.

Noun
nǐ kàn kan， zhè shì wǒ men de fēn bù tú
你 看 看 ， 这 是 我 们 的 **分 布** 图 。
You see, here's our **distribution** map.

239 分散　fēn sàn

Verb: to disperse; to be apart; to distract

bú yào fēn sàn zhù yì lì, yào jí zhōng
不要分散注意力, 要集中！
Don't get [your attention] **distracted**, be focused!

240 分手　fēn shǒu

Verb: to break up

fēn shǒu hòu, tā mǎ shàng jiù zhǎo le yí gè xīn nǚ péng yǒu
分手后, 他马上就找了一个新女朋友。
After **breaking up**, he immediately found a new girlfriend.

241 分为　fēn wéi

Verb: to divide into

qǐng bāng wǒ bǎ dàn gāo fēn wéi bā kuài
请帮我把蛋糕分为八块。
Please help me **divide** the cake **into** eight pieces.

242 分之　fēn zhī

used to express fractional numbers

dà gài sān fēn zhī yī de rén dào le
大概三分之一的人到了。
About **a third** of people arrived.

243 纷纷　fēn fēn

Adverb: one after another

dà jiā fēn fēn zǒu jìn le jiào táng
大家纷纷走进了教堂。
Everyone went into the church **one after another**.

244 奋斗   fèn dòu   **Verb:** to work hard
Noun: hard-work

Verb

wǒ yào wèi shí xiàn mù biāo bú duàn fèn dòu
我 要 为 实 现 目 标 不 断 **奋 斗** !
I will continue **to work hard** to achieve my goals!

Noun

wǒ xiāng xìn chí xù de fèn dòu shì yǒu yì yì de
我 相 信 持 续 的 **奋 斗** 是 有 意 义 的 。
I believe that continuous **hard-work** is worthwhile.

---

245 风格   fēng gé   **Noun:** style

wǒ hěn xǐ huān zhè jiàn qí páo de gǔ diǎn fēng gé
我 很 喜 欢 这 件 旗 袍 的 古 典 **风 格** 。
I really like the classical **style** of this cheongsam.

---

246 风景   fēng jǐng   **Noun:** scenery

zhè lǐ de fēng jǐng hěn měi měi nián xī yǐn hěn duō yóu kè
这 里 的 **风 景** 很 美 , 每 年 吸 引 很 多 游 客 。
The **scenery** here is beautiful and attracts many tourists yearly.

---

247 风俗   fēng sú   **Noun:** customs

duì le nǐ liǎo jiě dāng dì de fēng sú ma
对 了 , 你 了 解 当 地 的 **风 俗** 吗 ?
By the way, do you know the local **customs**?

---

248 封闭   fēng bì   **Verb:** to close

yóu yú shī gōng zhè tiáo lù bèi fēng bì le
由 于 施 工 , 这 条 路 被 **封 闭** 了 。
Due to construction, this road is **closed**.

249 否则   fǒu zé   **Conjunction:** otherwise

wǒ men rào dào ba， fǒu zé méi bàn fǎ guò qù
我 们 绕 道 吧， **否 则** 没 办 法 过 去。
Let's make a detour, **otherwise** we won't be able to get there.

250 夫妇   fū fù   **Noun:** married couple

jīn tiān shì zhè duì fū fù jié hūn zhōu nián de jì niàn rì
今 天 是 这 对 **夫 妇** 结 婚 50 周 年 的 纪 念 日。
Today marks this **couple**'s 50 year wedding anniversary.

251 夫妻   fū qī   **Noun:** man and wife

shèng jīng shàng shuō fū qī yào yí bèi zi ài duì fāng
圣 经 上 说 **夫 妻** 要 一 辈 子 爱 对 方。
The Bible says that **man and wife** should love each other throughout their lives.

252 夫人   fū rén   **Noun:** wife; madam (formal)

měi guó de dì yī fū rén hěn shòu huān yíng
美 国 的 第 一 **夫 人** 很 受 欢 迎。
The first **lady** of the United States is very popular.

253 符号   fú hào   **Noun:** mark; symbol

tā zài bái bǎn shàng huà le yí gè xīn xíng fú hào
她 在 白 板 上 画 了 一 个 心 形 **符 号**。
She drew a heart-shape **symbol** on the whiteboard.

254 符合   fú hé   **Verb:** to match; accord with

tā de jiào yù bèi jǐng fú hé wǒ men de yāo qiú
他 的 教 育 背 景 **符 合** 我 们 的 要 求。
His educational background **matches** our requirement.

255 付出　fù chū

Verb: to contribute; to sacrifice
Noun: contribution; sacrifice

Verb

fù mǔ wèi hái zi de chéng zhǎng fù chū le hěn duō
父 母 为 孩 子 的 成 长 **付 出** 了 很 多 。
Parents **sacrifice** a lot for their children's upbringing.

Noun

wǒ men yīng gāi gǎn jī tā men de fù chū
我 们 应 该 感 激 他 们 的 **付 出** 。
We should be grateful for their **contributions**.

256 负担　fù dān

Noun: burden

tā shī yè le suǒ yǐ jīng jì fù dān hěn zhòng
他 失 业 了 ， 所 以 经 济 **负 担** 很 重 。
He is unemployed, so the financial **burden** is heavy.

257 附近　fù jìn

Noun: nearby

nǐ jiā fù jìn yǒu kā fēi guǎn hé fàn guǎn ma
你 家 **附 近** 有 咖 啡 馆 和 饭 馆 吗 ？
Are there cafes and restaurants **nearby** your home?

258 复制　fù zhì

Verb: to copy

bǎ zhè jù huà fù zhì zhān tiē dào wén dàng
把 这 句 话 **复 制** 、 粘 贴 到 文 档 。
Copy and paste this sentence into a word document.

259 改善　gǎi shàn

Verb: to refine; to modify

zhāng jiào shòu jiàn yì wǒ gǎi shàn zhè piān lùn wén
张 教 授 建 议 我 **改 善** 这 篇 论 文 。
Professor Zhang suggested that I **modify** this essay.

260 改正　　gǎi zhèng　　**Verb: to correct**

wǒ jué de tā yīng gāi **gǎi zhèng** tā de huài pí qi
我 觉 得 他 应 该 **改 正** 他 的 坏 脾 气 。
I think he should **correct** his bad temper.

261 盖　　gài　　**Verb: to build; to cover**

qù zhǎo yí kuài bù **gài** shàng zhè tái gāng qín
去 找 一 块 布 **盖** 上 这 台 钢 琴 。
Go find a cloth **to cover** this piano.

262 概括　　gài kuò　　**Verb: to conclude; to summarize**

qǐng yòng yí jù huà **gài kuò** zhè gè xiǎo gù shì
请 用 一 句 话 **概 括** 这 个 小 故 事 。
Please **summarize** this short story in one sentence.

263 感兴趣　　gǎn xìng qù　　**Verb: to be interested in**

tā shì tóng xìng liàn ， duì nǚ rén bù **gǎn xìng qù**
他 是 同 性 恋 ， 对 女 人 不 **感 兴 趣** 。
He's gay and not **interested in** women.

264 高潮　　gāo cháo　　**Noun: peak; climax**

zhè bù diàn yǐng de **gāo cháo** fēi cháng zhèn hàn
这 部 电 影 的 **高 潮** 非 常 震 撼 ！
The **climax** of this movie is very shocking!

265 高价　　　gāo jià　　　**Noun:** high price

他 先 低 价 购 买 这 些 机 器 ， 然 后 **高 价**
tā xiān dī jià gòu mǎi zhè xiē jī qì rán hòu gāo jià
售 出 。
shòu chū

He first bought these machines at a low price and then sold them at a **high price**.

266 高尚　　　gāo shàng　　　**Adjective:** noble (morality)

我 以 前 觉 得 他 **高 尚** ， 现 在 发 现 他 很
wǒ yǐ qián jué de tā gāo shàng xiàn zài fā xiàn tā hěn
虚 伪 。
xū wěi

I used to think he was **noble**, but now I find him hypocritical.

267 高铁　　　gāo tiě　　　**Noun:** high-speed rail; high-speed train

跟 火 车 比 ， 我 更 喜 欢 坐 **高 铁** 。
gēn huǒ chē bǐ wǒ gèng xǐ huān zuò gāo tiě

Compared to the normal train, I prefer to take the **high-speed train**.

268 格外　　　gé wài　　　**Adverb:** especially

你 穿 上 这 条 裙 子 看 上 去 **格 外** 性 感 ！
nǐ chuān shàng zhè tiáo qún zi kàn shàng qù gé wài xìng gǎn

You look **especially** sexy in this dress!

269 隔(开)　　　gé kāi　　　**Verb:** to separate; to divide; space out

请 大 家 排 队 ， 互 相 **隔 开** 。
qǐng dà jiā pái duì hù xiāng gé kāi

Please line up and **space out** between each other.

270 个别   gè bié   **Adjective:** individual

nǐ kàn yǒu gè bié rén bù tīng zhǐ shì
你 看， 有 个 别 人 不 听 指 示。
You see, some **individual** people do not follow directions.

271 个体   gè tǐ   **Noun:** individual (business or legal term)

zhè xiàng fǎ lù jì bǎo hù gōng sī yòu bǎo hù gè tǐ
这 项 法 律 既 保 护 公 司， 又 保 护 个 体。
This law protects both corporations and **individuals**.

272 个性   gè xìng   **Noun:** personality

tā de gè xìng yòu dú tè yòu yǒu mèi lì
她 的 个 性 又 独 特 又 有 魅 力。
Her **personality** is unique and charming.

273 各个   gè gè   **Pronoun:** each

tā zài kǎo lù gè gè fāng miàn de lì bì
他 在 考 虑 各 个 方 面 的 利 弊。
He is considering the pros and cons of **each** aspect.

274 根   gēn   **Noun:** root

wǒ de zǔ guó shì wǒ de gēn dāng rán bù néng wàng jì
我 的 祖 国 是 我 的 根， 当 然 不 能 忘 记。
My motherland is my **root**, of course I can't forget it.

275 根据   gēn jù

Preposition: according to
Noun: basis; grounds

Pre.
gēn jù tā de jiě shì， zhè bú shì tā de cuò
根 据 他 的 解 释， 这 不 是 他 的 错 。
According to his explanation, it was not his fault.

Noun
kě shì， tā de shuō fǎ méi yǒu gēn jù
可 是， 他 的 说 法 没 有 根 据 。
However, his claim was unfounded (has no **grounds**).

276 工程   gōng chéng   **Noun:** engineering

tīng shuō zhè shì běi měi zuì dà de gōng chéng xiàng mù
听 说 这 是 北 美 最 大 的 工 程 项 目 。
I heard this is the largest **engineering** project in North America.

277 公元   gōng yuán   A.D.

wǒ de zēng zǔ fù chū shēng zài gōng yuán nián
我 的 曾 祖 父 出 生 在 公 元 1905 年 。
My great-grandfather was born in 1905 **A.D.**

278 供应   gōng yìng

Verb: to supply; to provide
Noun: supply

Verb
tā men fù zé gěi jūn duì gōng yìng shí wù hé zhuāng bèi
他 们 负 责 给 军 队 供 应 食 物 和 装 备 。
They are responsible for **supplying** food and equipment to the army.

Noun
wǒ men yí dìng yào bǎo hù zhè tiáo gōng yìng liàn
我 们 一 定 要 保 护 这 条 供 应 链 。
We must protect this **supply** chain.

279 共   gòng   **Verb:** to share; altogether (use with other words)

^{xiǎo} ^{shí} ^{hòu}   ^{wǒ} ^{hé} ^{wǒ} ^{mèi} ^{gòng} ^{xiǎng} ^{yí} ^{gè} ^{fáng} ^{jiān}
小 时 候 ， 我 和 我 妹 共 享 一 个 房 间 。
When I was a kid, my younger sister and I **shared** a room.

280 构成   gòu chéng   **Verb:** to form; to constitute; composed of

^{wǒ} ^{men} ^{de} ^{dà} ^{bù} ^{mén} ^{shì} ^{sān} ^{gè} ^{xiǎo} ^{bù} ^{mén} ^{gòu} ^{chéng} ^{de}
我 们 的 大 部 门 是 三 个 小 部 门 构 成 的 。
Our large department is **composed of** three small departments.

281 构造   gòu zào   **Noun:** structure; construction

^{qǐng} ^{gěi} ^{wǒ} ^{kàn} ^{yi} ^{kàn} ^{fáng} ^{zi} ^{de} ^{gòu} ^{zào} ^{tú}
请 给 我 看 一 看 房 子 的 构 造 图 。
Please show me the **construction** drawing of the house.

282 购买   gòu mǎi   **Verb:** to purchase

^{wǒ} ^{zài} ^{shāng} ^{chǎng} ^{gòu} ^{mǎi} ^{le} ^{yí} ^{tào} ^{shuì} ^{yī}
我 在 商 场 购 买 了 一 套 睡 衣 。
I **purchased** a set of pajamas at the mall.

283 购物   gòu wù   **Verb:** to go shopping

^{tā} ^{shì} ^{gè} ^{gòu} ^{wù} ^{kuáng}   ^{tiān} ^{tiān} ^{zài} ^{wǎng} ^{shàng} ^{gòu} ^{wù}
她 是 个 购 物 狂 ， 天 天 在 网 上 购 物 。
She is a shopaholic, and **goes shopping** online every day.

284 骨(头)   gǔ tou   **Noun:** bone

^{wǒ} ^{gěi} ^{wǒ} ^{de} ^{gǒu} ^{mǎi} ^{le} ^{yí} ^{gè} ^{gǔ} ^{tou} ^{wán} ^{jù}
我 给 我 的 狗 买 了 一 个 骨 头 玩 具 。
I bought a **bone** toy for my dog.

285 固定   gù dìng   **Adjective:** fixed

wǒ gēn yī shēng de yù yuē shí jiān shì gù dìng de
我 跟 医 生 的 预 约 时 间 是 **固 定** 的 。
My appointment time with the doctor is **fixed**.

286 瓜   guā   **Noun:** melon

zài xià tiān wǒ chāo xǐ huān chī xī guā
在 夏 天 ， 我 超 喜 欢 吃 西 **瓜** 。
In summer, I really like eating water**melon**.

287 怪   guài   **Adjective:** strange; odd
Adverb: quite; rather

Adj.

zhè gè rén jū rán zài shì zhōng xīn luǒ bēn zhēn guài
这 个 人 居 然 在 市 中 心 裸 奔 ！ 真 **怪** ！
This man is actually running naked in the city center! How **strange**!

Adv.

tā gāng gāng bèi jǐng chá zhuā le guài dǎo méi de
他 刚 刚 被 警 察 抓 了 ， **怪** 倒 霉 的 ！
He was just arrested by the police, **rather** unlucky!

288 关闭   guān bì   **Verb:** to close; to close down

hěn duō gōng sī yīn wèi qiàn zhài tài duō ér guān bì
很 多 公 司 因 为 欠 债 太 多 而 **关 闭** 。
Many companies **close down** because they owe too much debt.

289 关注   guān zhù   **Verb:** to follow (social media); to pay attention

rú guǒ nǐ xǐ huān qǐng guān zhù liú yán hé fēn xiǎng
如 果 你 喜 欢 ， 请 **关 注** 、 留 言 和 分 享 。
If you like it, please **follow**, comment and share it.

290 关于　　　　　guān yú　　　**Preposition:** about; regarding

guān yú xì tǒng wèn tí　zhuān jiā hái zài xiǎng bàn fǎ
关 于 系 统 问 题，专 家 还 在 想 办 法。
Regarding system issues, experts are still thinking of a method.

291 官　　　　　guān　　　**Noun:** official

tīng shuō tā shì lián hé guó de gāo guān
听 说 他 是 联 合 国 的 高 官。
I heard that he is a senior **official** of the United Nations.

292 官方　　　　guān fāng　　　**Adjective:** official
　　　　　　　　　　　　　　　　Noun: government side

Adj.
zhè shì wǒ men gōng sī de guān fāng wǎng zhàn
这 是 我 们 公 司 的 **官 方** 网 站。
This is the **official** website of our company.

Noun
guān fāng xīn wén bù yī dìng dōu shì zhēn de
官 方 新 闻 不 一 定 都 是 真 的。
News released by the **government side** is not necessarily always true.

293 光临　　　　guāng lín　　　**Verb:** to show presence (formal)

dà jiā hǎo　huān yíng guāng lín wǒ men de xué yuàn
大 家 好 ！欢 迎 **光 临** 我 们 的 学 院。
Hello everyone! Welcome (to **show presence**) to our academy.

294 光盘　　　　guāng pán　　　**Noun:** CD

wǒ wài gōng shōu jí le hěn duō yīn yuè guāng pán
我 外 公 收 集 了 很 多 音 乐 **光 盘**。
My maternal grandfather collected a lot of music **CDs**.

295 逛   guàng   **Verb:** to stroll

<small>wǒ men xǐ huān guàng dé guó de pí jiǔ jié</small>
我 们 喜 欢 **逛** 德 国 的 啤 酒 节 。
We love **strolling** at the beer festival in Germany.

296 归   guī   **Verb:** to return; go back (formal)

<small>tā guī guó hòu wǒ men zhǐ jiàn guò yí cì</small>
他 **归** 国 后 ， 我 们 只 见 过 一 次 。
After he **returned** to his home country, we only met once.

297 规律   guī lǜ   **Noun:** pattern (principle)

<small>sì jì gēng tì shì zì rán guī lǜ</small>
四 季 更 替 是 自 然 **规 律** 。
The change of seasons is nature's **pattern**.

298 规模   guī mó   **Noun:** scale

<small>gōng sī de guī mó yuè dà yuán gōng jiù yuè duō</small>
公 司 的 **规 模** 越 大 ， 员 工 就 越 多 。
The larger the company's **scale**, the more employees it has.

299 规则   guī zé   **Noun:** rule; regulation

<small>měi gè guó jiā dōu yǒu bù tóng de shè jiāo guī zé</small>
每 个 国 家 都 有 不 同 的 社 交 **规 则** 。
Every country has different social **rules**.

300 果实   guǒ shí   **Noun:** fruit (gain); good result

<small>zhè cì jù huì shì wèi le qìng zhù wǒ men de shèng lì guǒ shí</small>
这 次 聚 会 是 为 了 庆 祝 我 们 的 胜 利 **果 实** 。
This gathering is to celebrate the **fruits** of our victory.

301 过分   guò fèn

Adjective: go too far; too much (negative)
Adverb: excessively; overly

Adj.

shén me   tā zài jiē shàng mà nǐ   tài guò fèn
什么！他在街上骂你！太过分！
What! He scolded you on the street! He's **gone too far**!

Adv.

wǒ bà zǒng shì guò fèn qiáng diào yào shěng qián
我爸总是过分强调要省钱。
My dad always **overly** emphasizes saving money.

302 海水   hǎi shuǐ

Noun: brine; seawater

zhēn kě xī   zhè lǐ de hǎi shuǐ bèi wū rǎn le
真可惜，这里的海水被污染了。
It's a pity that the **seawater** here is polluted.

303 海鲜   hǎi xiān

Noun: seafood

wǒ yǐ jīng bàn nián méi yǒu chī hǎi xiān le
我已经半年没有吃海鲜了。
I haven't eaten **seafood** for half a year.

304 含   hán

Verb: to contain; to keep in mouth

jī dàn hán dàn bái zhì   yíng yǎng fēng fù
鸡蛋含蛋白质，营养丰富。
Eggs **contains** protein and are rich in nutrients.

nǐ kàn   wǒ de gǒu yòu zài hán shù zhī
你看，我的狗又在含树枝。
Look, my dog is **keeping** a branch **in** his **mouth** again.

305 含量   hán liàng

Noun: content (of quantity)

mǐ fàn de tàn shuǐ huà hé wù hán liàng gāo ma
米饭的碳水化合物含量高吗？
Does rice have high carbohydrate **content**?

306 含义　　hán yì　　**Noun:** significance; meaning

^{dìng}订 ^{hūn}婚 ^{jiè}戒 ^{zhǐ}指 ^{de}的 **^{hán}含 ^{yì}义** ^{duì}对 ^{tā}她 ^{hěn}很 ^{zhòng}重 ^{yào}要。

The **meaning** of the engagement ring is important to her.

307 含有　　hán yǒu　　**Verb:** to contain; to have

^{yīn}因 ^{wèi}为 ^{tā}它 **^{hán}含 ^{yǒu}有** ^{wèi}未 ^{hūn}婚 ^{fū}夫 ^{duì}对 ^{tā}她 ^{de}的 ^{ài}爱 ^{hé}和 ^{chéng}承 ^{nuò}诺。

Because it **contains** the love and commitment of her fiancé to her.

308 寒假　　hán jià　　**Noun:** the winter vacation/holiday

^{shǔ}暑 ^{jià}假 ^{bǐ}比 **^{hán}寒 ^{jià}假** ^{gèng}更 ^{zhí}值 ^{dé}得 ^{qī}期 ^{dài}待。

Summer holiday is more worth looking forward to than **winter holiday**.

309 寒冷　　hán lěng　　**Adjective:** cold; frigid; chill

^{zhè}这 ^{lǐ}里 ^{de}的 ^{dōng}冬 ^{tiān}天 ^{hěn}很 **^{hán}寒 ^{lěng}冷**，^{xià}夏 ^{tiān}天 ^{hěn}很 ^{yán}炎 ^{rè}热。

The winter here is very **cold** and the summer is very hot.

310 行业　　háng yè　　**Noun:** industry

^{lǚ}旅 ^{yóu}游 **^{háng}行 ^{yè}业** ^{shì}是 ^{dāng}当 ^{dì}地 ^{de}的 ^{jīng}经 ^{jì}济 ^{mìng}命 ^{mài}脉。

The tourism **industry** is the lifeblood of the local economy.

311 航班　　háng bān　　**Noun:** flight

^{nín}您 ^{hǎo}好！^{wǒ}我 ^{yào}要 ^{gǎi}改 ^{qiān}签 ^{wǒ}我 ^{de}的 **^{háng}航 ^{bān}班**。

Hello! I want to rebook my **flight**.

312 航空　　háng kōng　　**Noun:** aviation

zhè jiā háng kōng gōng sī de tóu zī zhě shì měi guó rén
这 家 **航 空** 公 司 的 投 资 者 是 美 国 人 。
The **aviation** company's investors are American.

313 毫米　　háo mǐ　　**Noun:** millimeter

yì lí mǐ děng yú shí háo mǐ
一 厘 米 等 于 十 **毫 米** 。
One centimeter equals to ten **millimeters**.

314 毫升　　háo shēng　　**Noun:** milliliter

yì shēng děng yú yì qiān háo shēng
一 升 等 于 一 千 **毫 升** 。
One liter equals to one thousand **milliliters**.

315 好友　　hǎo yǒu　　**Noun:** good friend

tā jiào zhāng hóng shì wǒ de duō nián hǎo yǒu
她 叫 张 红 ， 是 我 的 多 年 **好 友** 。
She is Zhang Hong, my **good friend** of many years.

316 号码　　hào mǎ　　**Noun:** number

zhè shì tā de shǒu jī hào mǎ tā huì zài jī chǎng děng nǐ
这 是 她 的 手 机 **号 码** ，她 会 在 机 场 等 你 。
This is her phone **number**, she will wait for you at the airport.

317 好　　hǎo　　**Adjective:** good; nice
Interjection: OK; alright

Adj.
tā de xìng gé hěn hǎo dài rén hěn rè qíng
她 的 性 格 很 **好** ， 待 人 很 热 情 。
She has a **good** personality and treats people very warmly.

Int.
hǎo wǒ yí dào jī chǎng jiù lián xì tā
好 ！我 一 到 机 场 就 联 系 她 。
OK! I will contact her as soon as I get to the airport.

318 合同　hé tong　**Noun:** contract

wǒ men xū yào bǎ hé tong fān yì chéng zhōng wén
我 们 需 要 把 **合 同** 翻 译 成 中 文 。
We need to translate the **contract** into Chinese.

319 黑暗　hēi àn　**Noun:** darkness　**Adjective:** dark

Noun
qí shí hēi àn yǔ guāng míng shì bìng cún de
其 实 ， **黑 暗** 与 光 明 是 并 存 的 。
In fact, **darkness** and light coexist.

Adj.
dì xià shì yòu hēi àn yòu cháo shī
地 下 室 又 **黑 暗** 又 潮 湿 。
The basement was **dark** and damp.

320 红包　hóng bāo　**Noun:** red packet

zài chūn jié wài gōng gěi le wǒ bā bǎi yuán hóng bāo
在 春 节 ， 外 公 给 了 我 八 百 元 **红 包** 。
In Chinese New Year, my grandpa gave me a **red packet** of ¥800.

321 后头　hòu tou　**Noun:** back

fáng zi de qián tou shì tíng chē chǎng hòu tou shì huā yuán
房 子 的 前 头 是 停 车 场 ， **后 头** 是 花 园 。
The front of the house is the parking lot and the **back** is the garden.

322 厚　hòu　**Adjective:** thick

wǒ xiǎng qù shāng chǎng mǎi yì xiē hòu nèi yī hé nèi kù
我 想 去 商 场 买 一 些 **厚** 内 衣 和 内 裤 。
I want to go to the mall to buy some **thick** underwear and briefs.

323 呼吸　hū xī　**Verb:** to breathe

zhè lǐ tài mēn wǒ yào chū qù hū xī xīn xiān kōng qì
这 里 太 闷 ， 我 要 出 去 **呼 吸** 新 鲜 空 气 。
It's too stuffy here, I'm going out **to breathe** fresh air.

324 忽视   hū shì   **Verb:** to ignore

tā de qíng shāng tài dī zǒng shì hū shì bié rén de gǎn shòu
他 的 情 商 太 低, 总 是 **忽 视** 别 人 的 感 受。
His EQ is too low, always **ignores** others' feelings.

325 户   hù   **Classifier** for households

zhè gè cūn zi yí gòng yǒu bā shí hù jū mín
这 个 村 子 一 共 有 八 十 **户** 居 民。
There are a total of eighty households in this village.

326 护士   hù shi   **Noun:** nurse

cūn lǐ de liáo yǎng yuàn yǒu qī gè hù shi
村 里 的 疗 养 院 有 七 个 **护 士**。
There are seven **nurses** in the care home in the village.

327 花   huā   **Noun:** flower; floral / **Verb:** to spend

Noun
wǒ xǐ huān zhè tiáo huā qún zi shàng miàn de huā hěn měi
我 喜 欢 这 条 **花** 裙 子, 上 面 的 **花** 很 美。
I like this **floral** skirt, the **flowers** on it are beautiful.

Verb
qún zi bù tài guì wǒ huā le sì shí měi yuán
裙 子 不 太 贵, 我 **花** 了 四 十 美 元。
The dress is not too expensive, I **spent** $40.

328 划   huá   **Verb:** to row; to scratch

zài xià tiān hěn duō rén zài hé shàng huá chuán
在 夏 天, 很 多 人 在 河 上 **划** 船。
In summer, many people **row** boats on the river.

329 划   huà   **Verb:** to delimit; to assign

zǒng cái bǎ zhè gè xiàng mù huà gěi shì chǎng bù mén le
总 裁 把 这 个 项 目 **划** 给 市 场 部 门 了。
The CEO **assigned** this project to the marketing department.

330 怀念   huái niàn   **Verb:** to yearn; to miss

wǒ men dōu fēi cháng huái niàn dà xué shēng huó
我 们 都 非 常 **怀 念** 大 学 生 活 。
We all **miss** our life in university very much.

331 怀疑   huái yí   **Verb:** to doubt; to suspect

wǒ huái yí zhè bú shì tā zhēn zhèng de mù dì
我 **怀 疑** 这 不 是 他 真 正 的 目 的 。
I **suspect** that's not his real purpose.

332 缓解   huǎn jiě   **Verb:** to relieve

kàn xǐ jù kě yǐ huǎn jiě shēng huó yā lì
看 喜 剧 可 以 **缓 解** 生 活 压 力 。
Watching comedy can **relieve** stress in life.

333 黄瓜   huáng guā   **Noun:** cucumber

wǒ bú ài chī huáng guā dàn ài chī xī guā hé dōng guā
我 不 爱 吃 **黄 瓜** ，但 爱 吃 西 瓜 和 冬 瓜 。
I don't like **cucumbers**, but I love watermelon and wax gourd.

334 黄金   huáng jīn   **Noun:** gold

wǒ de lǎo bǎn xǐ huān tóu zī huáng jīn hé shāng pǐn
我 的 老 板 喜 欢 投 资 **黄 金** 和 商 品 。
My boss likes to invest in **gold** and commodities.

335 回复   huí fù   **Verb:** to reply
Noun: reply

Verb

sān tiān le, tā hái shì méi yǒu huí fù wǒ de duǎn xìn
三 天 了 ， 他 还 是 没 有 **回 复** 我 的 短 信 。
It's been three days and he still hasn't **replied** to my message.

Noun

qí shí, tā de huí fù sù dù yì zhí hěn màn
其 实 ， 他 的 **回 复** 速 度 一 直 很 慢 。
In fact, his **reply** speed is always very slow.

336 汇   huì   **Verb:** to remit;
to gather together

wǒ měi nián dōu gěi guó wài de jiā rén huì kuǎn
我 每 年 都 给 国 外 的 家 人 **汇** 款 。
I **remit** money to my family abroad every year.

337 汇报   huì bào   **Verb:** to report
(job related)

wǒ měi gè yuè dǐ dōu yào xiàng jīng lǐ huì bào gōng zuò
我 每 个 月 底 都 要 向 经 理 **汇 报** 工 作 。
I always **report** work to my manager at the end of each month.

338 汇率   huì lǜ   **Noun:** exchange rate

zuì jìn huì lǜ bù wěn dìng, bú shì hé guó jì huì kuǎn
最 近 **汇 率** 不 稳 定 ， 不 适 合 国 际 汇 款 。
The **exchange rate** is unstable recently, unsuitable for
international remittances.

339 婚礼   hūn lǐ   **Noun:** wedding
ceremony

tā men dǎ suàn zài zhōng guó jǔ bàn yí gè zhōng shì hūn lǐ
他 们 打 算 在 中 国 举 办 一 个 中 式 **婚 礼** 。
They plan to hold a Chinese **wedding ceremony** in China.

340 火   huǒ   **Noun:** fire; flame
Adjective: popular

Noun

zhè dòng lóu de měi yì céng dōu yǒu miè huǒ qì
这 栋 楼 的 每 一 层 都 有 灭 火 器 。
There are **fire** extinguishers on every floor of the building.

Adj.

zhè bù diàn yǐng hěn huǒ piào fáng chāo guò shí yì měi yuán le
这 部 电 影 很 火 ，票 房 超 过 十 亿 美 元 了 ！
This movie is so **popular**, exceeding $1 billion at the box office!

341 伙   huǒ   **Noun:** buddy
(use with other words);
young guy

nà gè xiǎo huǒ yě shì wǒ men de huá xuě huǒ bàn
那 个 小 伙 也 是 我 们 的 滑 雪 伙 伴 。
That **young guy** is also our skiing **buddy**.

342 伙伴   huǒ bàn   **Noun:** partner;
mate; buddy

gōng sī zài ōu zhōu hé yà zhōu dōu yǒu shāng wù huǒ bàn
公 司 在 欧 洲 和 亚 洲 都 有 商 务 伙 伴 。
The company has business **partners** in Europe and Asia.

343 或许   huò xǔ   **Adverb:** maybe;
probably; perhaps

huò xǔ wǒ men kě yǐ zài zhōng guó zhǎo gōng yìng shāng
或 许 ，我 们 可 以 在 中 国 找 供 应 商 。
Perhaps, we can find suppliers in China.

344 货   huò   **Noun:** goods

wǎng shàng xiǎn shì mài jiā yǐ jīng fā huò le
网 上 显 示 卖 家 已 经 发 货 了 。
It shows online that the seller has shipped the **goods**.

345 获   huò   **Verb:** to reap (use with other words)

_{zhè cì chū chāi ràng wǒ shōu huò le bǎo guì de jīng yàn}
这 次 出 差 让 我 **收 获** 了 宝 贵 的 经 验 。
I **reaped** valuable experience from this business trip.

346 获得   huò dé   **Verb:** to obtain

_{wǒ yě huò dé le xīn de shāng wù rén mài}
我 也 **获 得** 了 新 的 商 务 人 脉 。
I also **obtained** new business contacts.

347 获奖   huò jiǎng   **Verb:** to win a prize; receive an award

_{tā zài zhè cì pǎo chē bǐ sài shàng huò jiǎng le}
他 在 这 次 跑 车 比 赛 上 **获 奖** 了 ！
He **won a prize** in this sports car race!

348 获取   huò qǔ   **Verb:** to gain

_{zhè tiáo guǎng gào bāng gōng sī huò qǔ le gāo lì rùn}
这 条 广 告 帮 公 司 **获 取** 了 高 利 润 。
This advertisement helped the company **gain** high profits.

349 几乎   jī hū   **Adverb:** almost

_{wǒ jī hū wàng le míng tiān shì wǒ gē de shēng rì}
我 **几 乎** 忘 了 明 天 是 我 哥 的 生 日 。
I **almost** forgot that tomorrow is my older brother's birthday.

350 机构   jī gòu   **Noun:** organization

_{tīng shuō wáng zǐ zàn zhù le èr shí duō jiā cí shàn jī gòu}
听 说 王 子 赞 助 了 二 十 多 家 慈 善 **机 构** 。
I heard that the prince has sponsored more than 20 charitiable **organizations**.

351 机遇   jī yù   **Noun:** opportunity (favorable)

chéng gōng de lù shàng yǒu jī yù， yě yǒu tiǎo zhàn
成 功 的 路 上 有 **机 遇**， 也 有 挑 战 。
On the road to success, there are **opportunities** and challenges.

352 积累   jī lěi   **Verb:** to accumulate / **Noun:** accumulation

Verb
zhè xiē nián tā jī lěi le hěn duō gōng zuò jīng yàn
这 些 年 他 **积 累** 了 很 多 工 作 经 验 。
He has **accumulated** a lot of work experience over the years.

Noun
zhè xiē jī lěi zēng zhǎng le tā de jiàn shí
这 些 **积 累** 增 长 了 他 的 见 识 。
These **accumulations** increased his knowledge.

353 激动   jī dòng   **Adjective:** excited

wǒ měi cì huí jiā， wǒ de gǒu dōu fēi cháng jī dòng
我 每 次 回 家， 我 的 狗 都 非 常 **激 动**。
Every time I come home, my dog always gets very **excited**.

354 激烈   jī liè   **Adjective:** fierce; heated

wǒ tīng shuō tā men de zhēng lùn fēi cháng jī liè
我 听 说 他 们 的 争 论 非 常 **激 烈** 。
I've heard their arguments were very **heated**.

355 及格   jí gé   **Verb:** to pass (exams)

hěn yí hàn， tā zhè cì de kǎo shì méi yǒu jí gé
很 遗 憾， 他 这 次 的 考 试 没 有 **及 格** 。
Unfortunately, he didn't **pass** the exam this time.

356 极   jí   **Adverb:** extremely; utmost

tā jí bú fù zé， bié zài gēn tā hé zuò
他 **极** 不 负 责， 别 再 跟 他 合 作 。
He is **extremely** irresponsible, don't cooperate with him again.

357 极其   jí qí   **Adverb:** extremely (formal)

zuì jìn gǔ shì jí qí bù wěn dìng wǒ bù xiǎng tóu zī
最 近 股 市 **极 其** 不 稳 定 ，我 不 想 投 资 。
The stock market is **extremely** unstable lately, I don't want to invest.

358 即将   jí jiāng   **Adverb:** about to; shortly

kāi mù shì jí jiāng kāi shǐ tā zhǔn bèi hǎo le ma
开 幕 式 **即 将** 开 始 ，他 准 备 好 了 吗 ？
The opening ceremony is **about to** begin, is he ready?

359 急忙   jí máng   **Adverb:** hastily; hurriedly

tā wàng le dài yǎn jiǎng gǎo jí máng qù bàn gōng shì zhǎo le
他 忘 了 带 演 讲 稿 ，**急 忙** 去 办 公 室 找 了 。
He forgot to bring his speech notes and **hurriedly** went to the office to find it.

360 集合   jí hé   **Verb:** to gather; to assemble

kuài diǎn wǒ men děi mǎ shàng zài huì yì shì jí hé
快 点 ！我 们 得 马 上 在 会 议 室 **集 合** 。
Hurry up! We must **assemble** in the conference room immediately.

361 记载   jì zǎi   **Verb:** to record (experience/history)   **Noun:** record

Verb
zhè xiē dàng àn jì zǎi le tā de chéng gōng yǔ shī bài
这 些 档 案 **记 载** 了 他 的 成 功 与 失 败 。
These archives **recorded** his successes and failures.

Noun
zhè xiē jì zǎi duì wǒ men de yán jiū hěn yǒu yòng
这 些 **记 载** 对 我 们 的 研 究 很 有 用 。
These **records** are very useful for our research.

362 纪律   jì lǜ   **Noun:** discipline

yǒu xiē hái zi tài pàn nì   bù zūn shǒu jì lǜ
有 些 孩 子 太 叛 逆 ， 不 遵 守 **纪 律** 。
Some children are too rebellious and don't follow **discipline**.

363 技巧   jì qiǎo   **Noun:** skill

qǐng gěi wǒ tuī jiàn yì běn guān yú guǎn lǐ jì qiǎo de shū
请 给 我 推 荐 一 本 关 于 管 理 **技 巧** 的 书 。
Please recommend me a book on management **skills**.

364 系   xì   **Noun:** department (academic)

zhāng wén shì kē xué xì de fù jiào shòu
张 文 是 科 学 **系** 的 副 教 授 。
Zhang Wen is an associate professor in the **Department** of Science.

365 季   jì   **Noun:** season (use with other words)

wǒ zuì ài chūn jì tā zuì ài qiū jì
我 最 爱 **春 季** ， 他 最 爱 **秋 季** 。
I love **spring** the most, and he loves **autumn** the most.

366 季节   jì jié   **Noun:** season

zhè gè jì jié de qì hòu tài gān zào nǐ yào duō hē shuǐ
这 个 **季 节** 的 气 候 太 干 燥 ， 你 要 多 喝 水 。
The climate is too dry this **season**, you need to drink more water.

367 季度   jì dù   **Noun:** quarter (of a year)

wǒ fù zé xiě gōng sī de jì dù bào gào
我 负 责 写 公 司 的 **季 度** 报 告 。
I am in charge of writing the company's **quarterly** reports.

368 既　　jì　　**Conjunction:** and; as well as (既...又...)

zhè gè rèn wù **jì** fù zá **yòu** fèi shí jiān
这 个 任 务 **既** 复 杂 **又** 费 时 间 。
This task is complex **and** time-consuming.

369 既然　　jì rán　　**Conjunction:** as; since

jì rán nǐ yā lì dà jiù xiū jià liǎng tiān ba
既 然 你 压 力 大 ， 就 休 假 两 天 吧 。
Since you're stressed, I suggest you take two days off.

370 寄　　jì　　**Verb:** to post

wǒ dǎ suàn gěi nǚ péng yǒu **jì** yì hé qiǎo kè lì
我 打 算 给 女 朋 友 **寄** 一 盒 巧 克 力 。
I plan **to post** a box of chocolates to my girlfriend.

371 加班　　jiā bān　　**Verb:** to work overtime

wǒ zuì jìn zǒng shì **jiā bān** méi shí jiān kàn tā
我 最 近 总 是 **加 班** ， 没 时 间 看 她 。
I always **work overtime** recently, no time to see her.

372 加入　　jiā rù　　**Verb:** to join; become a member

wǒ xiǎng shēn qǐng **jiā rù** nǐ men de jù lè bù
我 想 申 请 **加 入** 你 们 的 俱 乐 部 。
I would like to apply **to join** your club.

373 加油站　　jiā yóu zhàn　　**Noun:** gas station

zhè gè **jiā yóu zhàn** de shōu fèi tài gāo wǒ men qù xià
这 个 **加 油 站** 的 收 费 太 高 ， 我 们 去 下
yí gè
一 个 。
This **gas station** charges too much, let's go to the next one.

374 家务　　　jiā wù　　　**Noun:** housework

他 老 婆 是 全 职 太 太 ， 只 做 家 务 。
tā lǎo pó shì quán zhí tài tai zhǐ zuò jiā wù
His wife is a full-time wife and only does **housework**.

375 假如　　　jiǎ rú　　　**Conjunction:** if (supposing)

假 如 他 破 产 ， 他 们 就 会 失 去 经 济 来 源 。
jiǎ rú tā pò chǎn tā men jiù huì shī qù jīng jì lái yuán
If he goes bankrupt, they lose their financial sources.

376 坚固　　　jiān gù　　　**Adjective:** strong (material)

这 栋 房 子 很 坚 固 ， 没 有 被 地 震 破 坏 。
zhè dòng fáng zi hěn jiān gù méi yǒu bèi dì zhèn pò huài
This house is **strong** and was not damaged by the earthquake.

377 检测　　　jiǎn cè　　　**Verb:** to check; to examine (for issues)　**Noun:** inspection

Verb
我 们 团 队 在 检 测 产 品 的 质 量 。
wǒ men tuán duì zài jiǎn cè chǎn pǐn de zhì liàng
Our team is **examining** the quality of the product.

Noun
这 是 质 量 检 测 报 告 ， 请 看 一 下 。
zhè shì zhì liàng jiǎn cè bào gào qǐng kàn yi xià
This is the quality **inspection** report, please take a look.

378 减　　　jiǎn　　　**Verb:** to subtract; to diminish

过 了 热 恋 期 ， 他 的 激 情 就 减 了 。
guò le rè liàn qī tā de jī qíng jiù jiǎn le
After passing the passionate love period, his passion **diminished**.

379 减肥　　　jiǎn féi　　　**Verb:** to lose weight

zhǎng pàng hòu　péng yǒu men dōu shuō wǒ yīng gāi jiǎn féi
长 胖 后 ， 朋 友 们 都 说 我 应 该 减 肥 。
After gaining weight, my friends all said I should **lose weight**.

380 减少　　　jiǎn shǎo　　　**Verb:** to reduce

wǒ jiàn yì nǐ zài yǐn shí shàng jiǎn shǎo kuài cān
我 建 议 你 在 饮 食 上 减 少 快 餐 。
I suggest you **reduce** fast food in your diet.

381 简历　　　jiǎn lì　　　**Noun:** resume; CV

tā bāng wǒ xiě le yì zhāng wán měi de jiǎn lì
他 帮 我 写 了 一 张 完 美 的 简 历 。
He helped me write a perfect **resume**.

382 健身　　　jiàn shēn　　　**Verb:** to workout

tā měi tiān zǎo shàng dōu qù jiàn shēn fáng jiàn shēn
他 每 天 早 上 都 去 健 身 房 健 身 。
He always goes to the gym every morning **to workout**.

383 渐渐　　　jiàn jiàn　　　**Adverb:** gradually; step by step

tā jiàn jiàn yǒu le jǐ ròu hěn yǒu nán rén wèi
他 渐 渐 有 了 肌 肉 ， 很 有 男 人 味 。
He **gradually** gained muscle, and is very masculine.

384 江　　　jiāng　　　**Noun:** river

cháng jiāng shì zhōng guó zuì chū míng de yì tiáo jiāng
长 江 是 中 国 最 出 名 的 一 条 江 。
The Yangtze **River** is the most famous **river** in China.

385 讲究 — jiǎng jiu

Verb: to stress; be particular about

wǒ tài tai zài chuān yī fāng miàn hěn jiǎng jiu
我 太 太 在 穿 衣 方 面 很 **讲 究** 。
My wife **is** very **particular about** dressing.

386 讲座 — jiǎng zuò

Noun: lecture

zhè gè jiǎng zuò zhēn wú liáo， nǐ bù jué de ma
这 个 **讲 座** 真 无 聊， 你 不 觉 得 吗 ？
This **lecture** is really boring, don't you think so?

387 奖 — jiǎng

Noun: award; prize; reward

wǒ tīng shuō tā de lùn wén huò jiǎng le！ zhēn bàng
我 听 说 他 的 论 文 获 **奖** 了 ！ 真 棒 ！
I heard he won an **award** for his thesis! So awesome!

388 奖金 — jiǎng jīn

Noun: bonus

wǒ zài nián dǐ huò dé le yí wàn yuán de jiǎng jīn
我 在 年 底 获 得 了 一 万 元 的 **奖 金** 。
I got a **bonus** of 10,000 yuan at the end of the year.

389 奖学金 — jiǎng xué jīn

Noun: scholarship

shēn qǐng jiǎng xué jīn de tiáo jiàn shì shén me
申 请 **奖 学 金** 的 条 件 是 什 么 ？
What are the conditions for applying for the **scholarship**?

390 降 — jiàng

Verb: to drop; to descend

tài hǎo le！ fáng jià zhōng yú jiàng le
太 好 了 ！ 房 价 终 于 **降** 了 ！
Great! House prices finally **dropped**!

391 降低　jiàng dī　**Verb:** to reduce

wǒ men yào xiǎng bàn fǎ jiàng dī shēng chǎn chéng běn
我 们 要 想 办 法 **降 低** 生 产 成 本 。
We need to find ways **to reduce** production costs.

392 降价　jiàng jià　**Verb:** to reduce price

jīn tiān shāng diàn dǎ zhé hěn duō shāng pǐn dōu jiàng jià le
今 天 商 店 打 折 ，很 多 商 品 都 **降 价** 了 。
The store is having a sale (discounting) today; many items are **reduced in price.**

393 降落　jiàng luò　**Verb:** to land

wǒ de fēi jī jiǔ diǎn qǐ fēi shí èr diǎn jiàng luò
我 的 飞 机 九 点 起 飞 ， 十 二 点 **降 落** 。
My plane takes off at nine and **lands** at twelve.

394 降温　jiàng wēn　**Verb:** to lower the temperature

zuó wǎn xià dà bào yǔ hòu jiù jiàng wēn le
昨 晚 下 大 暴 雨 后 就 **降 温** 了 。
The **temperature** was **lowered** after heavy rain last night.

395 交换　jiāo huàn　**Verb:** to exchange

wǒ zàn shí hé lín jū jiāo huàn le tíng chē wèi
我 暂 时 和 邻 居 **交 换** 了 停 车 位 。
I temporarily **exchanged** parking spaces with my neighbor.

396 交际　jiāo jì　**Noun:** communication; social interaction

tā de dà xué zhuān yè shì kuà wén huà jiāo jì
她 的 大 学 专 业 是 跨 文 化 **交 际** 。
Her college major is Intercultural **Communication.**

397 教授   jiào shòu   **Noun:** professor

wǒ men xué yuàn yǒu shí míng jiào shòu hé èr shí míng jiǎng shī
我 们 学 院 有 十 名 **教 授** 和 二 十 名 讲 师 。
Our college has ten **professors** and twenty lecturers.

398 教训   jiào xùn   **Noun:** lesson (learned from bad experience)

zhè cì shī bài gěi le wǒ hěn dà de jiào xùn
这 次 失 败 给 了 我 很 大 的 **教 训** ！
This failure has taught me a big **lesson**!

399 阶段   jiē duàn   **Noun:** stage (time period or process)

rén shēng de bù tóng jiē duàn yǒu bù tóng de tiǎo zhàn
人 生 的 不 同 **阶 段** 有 不 同 的 挑 战 。
Different **stages** of life have different challenges.

400 街(道)   jiē dào   **Noun:** street

zhè tiáo jiē dào shàng de hěn duō shāng diàn dōu dǎo bì le
这 条 **街 道** 上 的 很 多 商 店 都 倒 闭 了 。
Many shops on this **street** are closed down.

401 (节)省   jié shěng   **Verb:** to save (opposite to waste)

zuò fēi jī bǐ zuò huǒ chē gèng jié shěng shí jiān
坐 飞 机 比 坐 火 车 更 **(节) 省** 时 间 。
Traveling by plane is more time-**saving** than taking the train.

402 结   jié   **Verb:** to form; to knot

zuó wǎn xià dà xuě lù shàng jié le yì céng xuě
昨 晚 下 大 雪 ， 路 上 **结** 了 一 层 雪 。
It snowed heavily last night; a layer of snow **formed** on the road.

403 结构   jié gòu   **Noun:** structure

zhè shì fáng zi de jié gòu tú nǐ jué de zěn me yàng
这 是 房 子 的 **结 构** 图，你 觉 得 怎 么 样？
Here is the **structure** drawing of the house, what do you think?

404 结论   jié lùn   **Noun:** conclusion

wǒ men de tǎo lùn zàn shí méi yǒu dé chū jié lùn
我 们 的 讨 论 暂 时 没 有 得 出 **结 论** 。
Our discussions have not yet reached a **conclusion**.

405 姐妹   jiě mèi   **Noun:** sisters

wǒ mā yǒu liǎng gè jiě mèi hé sān gè xiōng dì
我 妈 有 两 个 **姐 妹** 和 三 个 兄 弟 。
My mother has two **sisters** and three brothers.

406 解释   jiě shì   **Verb:** to explain
Noun: explanation

Verb
qǐng nǐ jiě shì zhè cì tán pàn shī bài de yuán yīn
请 你 **解 释** 这 次 谈 判 失 败 的 原 因 。
Please **explain** the reason of this negotiation failure.

Noun
xiè xie nǐ de jiě shì wǒ zhōng yú míng bái le
谢 谢 你 的 **解 释**，我 终 于 明 白 了 。
Thank you for your **explanation**, I finally understand.

407 尽快   jǐn kuài   **Adverb:** as soon as possible

wǒ men yào jǐn kuài xiǎng bàn fǎ jiě jué zhè gè wèn tí
我 们 要 **尽 快** 想 办 法 解 决 这 个 问 题 。
We need to find a way to solve this problem **as soon as possible**.

408 紧密 jǐn mì **Adjective:** close; inseparable

bǎo chí jǐn mì de hé zuò guān xi hěn zhòng yào
保持**紧密**的合作关系很重要。
It is important to maintain a **close** partnership.

409 尽力 jìn lì **Adverb:** try one's best

wǒ huì jǐn lì zài sān tiān nèi wán chéng rèn wù
我会**尽力**在三天内完成任务。
I will **try my best** to finish the task in three days.

410 进口 jìn kǒu **Verb:** to import

zhè xiē kā fēi dòu shì cóng nán měi zhōu jìn kǒu de
这些咖啡豆是从南美洲**进口**的。
These coffee beans are **imported** from South America.

411 近代 jìn dài **Noun:** modern times

jìn chū kǒu háng yè shì jìn dài de zhòng yào háng yè
进出口行业是**近代**的重要行业。
The import-export industry is an important industry in **modern times**.

412 禁止 jìn zhǐ **Verb:** to ban; to prohibit

cóng qù nián qǐ wǒ bà jiù bèi wǒ mā jìn zhǐ dǔ bó le
从去年起，我爸就被我妈**禁止**赌博了。
Since last year, my dad has been **banned** from gambling by my mom.

413 经典 jīng diǎn **Noun:** classic

duì le nǐ zuì xǐ huān de jīng diǎn diàn yǐng shì shén me
对了，你最喜欢的**经典**电影是什么？
By the way, what is your favorite **classic** movie?

414 精力   jīng lì   **Noun:** energy (effort)

wǒ lǎo gōng tài máng   méi yǒu jīng lì guǎn hái zi
我 老 公 太 忙 ， 没 有 精 力 管 孩 子 。
My husband is too busy, so has no **energy** to take care of kids.

415 竟然   jìng rán   **Adverb:** shockingly; unexpectedly

tā jìng rán yǒu xiǎo sān   wǒ yǐ wéi tā shì gè hǎo lǎo gōng
他 竟 然 有 小 三 ！ 我 以 为 他 是 个 好 老 公 。
Unexpectedly he has a mistress! I thought he was a good husband.

416 镜头   jìng tóu   **Noun:** camera lens; shot (scene)

zhè gè jiē wěn jìng tóu shì diàn yǐng de gāo cháo
这 个 接 吻 镜 头 是 电 影 的 高 潮 。
This kissing **scene** is the climax of the movie.

417 镜子   jìng zi   **Noun:** mirror

wǒ xiàn zài yào huà zhuāng   xū yào yí miàn xiǎo jìng zi
我 现 在 要 化 妆 ， 需 要 一 面 小 镜 子 。
I want to put on makeup now and need a small **mirror**.

418 究竟   jiū jìng   **Adverb:** exactly (for questions)

wǒ xiǎng zhī dào   nǐ jiū jìng zài dān xīn shén me
我 想 知 道 ， 你 究 竟 在 担 心 什 么 ？
I want to know, what **exactly** are you worried about?

419 酒吧   jiǔ bā   **Noun:** bar

zhè gè jiǔ bā hěn chū míng   yǒu yì bǎi nián de lì shǐ
这 个 酒 吧 很 出 名 ， 有 一 百 年 的 历 史 。
This **bar** is very famous and has a history of 100 years.

420 居民　　　jū mín　　**Noun:** resident

dāng dì de jū mín dōu xǐ huān qù nà lǐ hē jiǔ
当 地 的 **居 民** 都 喜 欢 去 那 里 喝 酒 。
Local **residents** all like to go there to drink.

421 (居)住　　　jū zhù　　**Verb:** to live

tuì xiū hòu wǒ xiǎng bān dào xiāng xià jū zhù
退 休 后 ， 我 想 搬 到 乡 下 (居) **住** 。
After retirement, I want to move to the countryside **to live**.

422 局　　　jú　　**Noun:** bureau; gathering

wǒ dà gē zài jǐng chá jú gōng zuò le wǔ nián
我 大 哥 在 警 察 **局** 工 作 了 五 年 。
My eldest brother worked in the police **bureau** for 5 years.

wǒ píng jūn měi gè yuè yǒu sān gè fàn jú
我 平 均 每 个 月 有 三 个 饭 **局** 。
On average I have three dinner **gatherings** a month.

423 巨大　　　jù dà　　**Adjective:** huge

zhè gè xiàng mù de yù suàn tài jù dà kǒng pà bù xíng
这 个 项 目 的 预 算 太 **巨 大** ， 恐 怕 不 行 。
The budget for this project is too **huge**, I'm afraid it won't work.

424 具备　　　jù bèi　　**Verb:** to possess; to have (formal)

wǒ men gōng sī hái bú jù bèi zhè me gāo de cháng
我 们 公 司 还 不 **具 备** 这 么 高 的 偿
huán néng lì
还 能 力 。
Our company does not **have** such a high repayment ability.

425 距离   jù lí   **Noun: distance**

duì yú zhēn ài, shí jiān hé jù lí dōu bú shì wèn tí
对 于 真 爱，时 间 和 **距 离** 都 不 是 问 题 。
For true love, time and **distance** are both not problems.

426 聚   jù   **Verb: to assemble; to gather**

yǒu jǐ qiān rén jù zài shì zhōng xīn kàng yì
有 几 千 人 **聚** 在 市 中 心 抗 议 。
Thousands of people are **gathering** in the city center to protest.

427 聚会   jù huì   **Noun: party; gathering**

wǒ shàng zhōu cān jiā le guī mì de shēng rì jù huì
我 上 周 参 加 了 闺 蜜 的 生 日 **聚 会** 。
I went to attend my best friend's birthday **party** last week.

428 卷   juǎn   **Adjective: curly** / **Noun: roll**

Adj.
tā shì gè jīn fà měi nǚ, tóu fa yǒu diǎn juǎn
她 是 个 金 发 美 女，头 发 有 点 **卷** 。
She is a beautiful blonde; her hair is a bit **curly**.

Noun
tā gěi wǒ men zuò le chūn juǎn hé shòu sī juǎn
她 给 我 们 做 了 春 **卷** 和 寿 司 **卷** 。
She made us spring **rolls** and sushi **rolls**.

429 卷   juàn   **Noun: file; volume;**

guān yú zhè chǎng zhàn zhēng, tú shū guǎn yǒu jǐ juàn jì lù
关 于 这 场 战 争，图 书 馆 有 几 **卷** 记 录 。
Regarding this war, the library has several **volumes** of records.

430 角色　　　jué sè　　　**Noun:** role; character

hěn duō nǚ yǎn yuán xǐ huān bái xuě gōng zhǔ de jué sè
很 多 女 演 员 喜 欢 白 雪 公 主 的 **角 色**。
Many actresses love the **role** of Snow White.

431 开花　　　kāi huā　　　**Verb:** to flower; to bloom

tài bàng le ! wǒ de mǔ dān zhōng yú kāi huā le
太 棒 了 ！ 我 的 牡 丹 终 于 **开 花** 了 ！
Awesome! My peonies are finally **blooming**.

432 开水　　　kāi shuǐ　　　**Noun:** boiling water

rú guǒ nǐ yòng kāi shuǐ zhǔ fàn　　　fēn zhōng jiù hǎo
如 果 你 用 **开 水** 煮 饭 ，20 分 钟 就 好 。
If you cook rice in **boiling water**, it will be done in 20 minutes.

433 看不起　　　kàn bu qǐ　　　**Verb:** to despise; to look down upon

tā shì yì wàn fù wēng kàn bu qǐ pián yi de lǐ wù
他 是 亿 万 富 翁 ， **看 不 起** 便 宜 的 礼 物 。
He's a billionaire who **despises** cheap gifts.

434 看来　　　kàn lái　　　**Adverb:** it seems; it appears

kàn lái tā shì gè hěn fū qiǎn de fù rén
看 来 他 是 个 很 肤 浅 的 富 人 ！
It seems that he is a very superficial rich man!

435 看(望)　　　kàn wàng　　　**Verb:** to visit (people)

wǒ měi nián dōu qù sū gé lán kàn wàng wǒ de wài pó
我 每 年 都 去 苏 格 兰 **看 望** 我 的 外 婆 。
I always go to **visit** my maternal grandma in Scotland every year.

436 考察 kǎo chá **Verb:** to examine; to inspect

kē xué jiā tuán duì zài běi jí kǎo chá bīng chuān
科学家团队在北极考察冰川。
A team of scientists are **examining** glaciers in the Arctic.

437 考虑 kǎo lǜ **Verb:** to consider

hěn bào qiàn wǒ xū yào liǎng tiān shí jiān kǎo lǜ zhè jiàn shì
很抱歉，我需要两天时间考虑这件事。
Sorry, I need two days **to consider** this matter.

438 棵 kē **Classifier** for trees

tā men gāng gāng zài huā yuán zhòng le wǔ kē táo shù
他们刚刚在花园种了五棵桃树。
They just planted five peach trees in the garden.

439 可见 kě jiàn **Conjunction:** so; it can be seen that

kě jiàn tā men fēi cháng xǐ huān táo huā
可见，他们非常喜欢桃花。
It can be seen that they like peach blossoms very much.

440 空间 kōng jiān **Noun:** space

kàn lái wǒ de diàn nǎo nèi cún kōng jiān bú gòu
看来我的电脑内存空间不够。
It seems that my computer does not have enough storage **space**.

441 空 kōng **Adjective:** empty

hǎo qí guài wèi shén me zhè gè wén jiàn jiā shì kōng de
好奇怪！为什么这个文件夹是空的？
How weird! Why is this folder **empty**?

442 口袋　　kǒu dài　　**Noun:** pocket

zhè tiáo kù zi de kǒu dài tài xiǎo　zhuāng bù liǎo shǒu jī
这 条 裤 子 的 **口 袋** 太 小 ， 装 不 了 手 机 。
These trouser **pockets** are too small to fit a mobile phone.

443 口语　　kǒu yǔ　　**Noun:** spoken language

wǒ měi tiān zǎo shàng liàn xí yí gè xiǎo shí de zhōng wén kǒu yǔ
我 每 天 早 上 练 习 一 个 小 时 的 中 文 **口 语** 。
I practice **spoken** Chinese for an hour every morning.

444 苦　　kǔ　　**Adjective:** bitter

kǔ guā hěn kǔ　fēng mì hěn tián
苦 瓜 很 **苦** ， 蜂 蜜 很 甜 。
Bitter melon is **bitter**, honey is sweet.

445 会计　　kuài jì　　**Noun:** accountant

qí shí　zhè gè kuài jì de jīng yàn fēi cháng fēng fù
其 实 ， 这 个 **会 计** 的 经 验 非 常 丰 富 ！
In fact, this **accountant** has very rich experience!

446 快递　　kuài dì　　**Noun:** delivery

jīn tiān xià wǔ wǒ děi zài jiā děng yí gè guó jì kuài dì
今 天 下 午 我 得 在 家 等 一 个 国 际 **快 递** 。
I have to wait for an international **delivery** at home this afternoon.

447 宽　　kuān　　**Adjective:** wide

tā de jiān bǎng yǒu diǎn kuān　suǒ yǐ mǎi chèn shān bù róng yì
他 的 肩 膀 有 点 **宽** ， 所 以 买 衬 衫 不 容 易 。
His shoulders are a bit **wide**, so it's not easy to buy shirts.

448 宽广　　kuān guǎng　　**Adjective:** broad; vast; extensive

tā yǐ qián xīn xiōng kuān guǎng，xiàn zài xīn xiōng xiá zhǎi
他 以 前 心 胸 **宽 广**，现 在 心 胸 狭 窄。
He was **broad**-minded before, but now narrow-minded.

449 矿泉水　　kuàng quán shuǐ　　**Noun:** mineral water

shén me！zhè lǐ de kuàng quán shuǐ shí měi yuán yì píng
什 么！这 里 的 **矿 泉 水** 十 美 元 一 瓶？
What! The **mineral water** here is ten dollars a bottle?

450 扩大　　kuò dà　　**Verb:** to expand

jǐng chá men dǎ suàn kuò dà sōu chá fàn wéi
警 察 们 打 算 **扩 大** 搜 查 范 围。
The police plan **to expand** the scope of the search.

451 扩展　　kuò zhǎn　　**Verb:** to extend; to expand

gōng sī xiǎng bǎ zhè kuǎn ruǎn jiàn kuò zhǎn dào yà zhōu shì chǎng
公 司 想 把 这 款 软 件 **扩 展** 到 亚 洲 市 场。
The company wants **to expand** the software into the Asian market.

452 括号　　kuò hào　　**Noun:** brackets

wǒ kàn de dǒng，yīn wèi kuò hào lǐ yǒu jiě shì
我 看 得 懂，因 为 **括 号** 里 有 解 释。
I can understand it because the explanation is in the **brackets**.

453 垃圾　　lā jī　　**Noun:** garbage; waste; refuse; rubbish

bō li píng shì kě yǐ huí shōu de lā jī
玻 璃 瓶 是 可 以 回 收 的 **垃 圾**。
Glass bottles are recyclable **garbage**.

454 拉开   lā kāi   **Verb:** to pull open; to draw back

qǐng nǐ bāng wǒ lā kāi chuāng lián, rán hòu dǎ kāi chuāng hu
请 你 帮 我 **拉 开** 窗 帘， 然 后 打 开 窗 户。
Please help me **pull open** the curtain, then open the window.

455 辣   là   **Adjective:** spicy

wǒ men dōu ài chī sì chuān huǒ guō, yòu má yòu là
我 们 都 爱 吃 四 川 火 锅， 又 麻 又 **辣**！
We all love Sichuan hotpot, both numbing and **spicy**!

456 来不及   lái bu jí   **Verb:** too late; not enough time

biǎo yǎn kuài jié shù le, kǒng pà wǒ men lái bu jí guān kàn
表 演 快 结 束 了， 恐 怕 我 们 **来 不 及** 观 看。
The show is ending soon; I'm afraid we'll be **too late** to watch it.

457 来得及   lái de jí   **Verb:** there's still time

bié dān xīn, rú guǒ wǒ men dǎ chē qù, jiù lái de jí
别 担 心， 如 果 我 们 打 车 去， 就 **来 得 及**。
Don't worry, if we take a taxi, **there's still time**.

458 来源   lái yuán   **Noun:** source

dì èr cì shì jiè dà zhàn shì zhè bù diàn yǐng de lái yuán
第 二 次 世 界 大 战 是 这 部 电 影 的 **来 源**。
World War II is the **source** of this movie.

459 老公   lǎo gōng   **Noun:** husband (colloquial)

tā lǎo gōng shì zhè jiā dà gōng sī de hé zuò huǒ bàn
她 **老 公** 是 这 家 大 公 司 的 合 作 伙 伴。
Her **husband** is a business partner of this big company.

460 老婆　lǎo pó　**Noun:** wife (colloquial)

wǒ tīng shuō tā lǎo pó shì gāo jí jiào yù gù wèn
我 听 说 他 **老 婆** 是 高 级 教 育 顾 问 。

I heard his **wife** is a senior education consultant.

461 老家　lǎo jiā　**Noun:** hometown

wǒ de lǎo jiā zài běi jīng， tā de lǎo jiā zài dōng jīng
我 的 **老 家** 在 北 京 ， 她 的 **老 家** 在 东 京 。

My **hometown** is in Beijing, her **hometown** is in Tokyo.

462 老实　lǎo shi　**Adjective:** honest (colloquial)

zhè gè chú shī yòu lǎo shi yòu kě kào
这 个 厨 师 又 **老 实** 又 可 靠 。

This chef is **honest** and reliable.

463 乐趣　lè qù　**Noun:** pleasure; entertainment

tā píng shí méi shén me ài hào， wéi yī de lè qù
他 平 时 没 什 么 爱 好 ， 唯 一 的 **乐 趣**
shì dǎ pái
是 打 牌 。

He usually has no hobbies, his only **pleasure** is playing cards.

464 泪　lèi　**Noun:** teardrop; tear

wǒ kàn dào tā de zuǒ yǎn liú le yì dī lèi
我 看 到 他 的 左 眼 流 了 一 滴 **泪** 。

I saw a **teardrop** flow from his left eye.

465 泪水 　　　lèi shuǐ　　　**Noun:** tears

qí shí zhè shì wǒ dì yī cì kàn dào tā de lèi shuǐ
其实，这是我第一次看到他的**泪水**。
In fact, this is the first time I saw his **tears**.

466 类型 　　　lèi xíng　　　**Noun:** type

wǒ xiǎng zhī dào nǐ xǐ huān shén me lèi xíng de nán péng yǒu
我想知道你喜欢什么**类型**的男朋友。
I want to know what **type** of boyfriend you like.

467 冷静 　　　lěng jìng　　　**Verb:** to calm down
　　　　　　　　　　　　　　　　Adjective: calm

Verb
qǐng lěng jìng xiān zuò xià hǎo hǎo xiǎng yi xiǎng
请**冷静**，先坐下，好好想一想。
Please **calm down**, sit down and think about it well.

Adj.
tā yǐ qián hěn bào zào xiàn zài bǐ jiào lěng jìng
他以前很暴躁，现在比较**冷静**。
He used to be very irritable, but now he is relatively **calm**.

468 厘米 　　　lí mǐ　　　**Noun:** centimeter

tā de yāo wéi shì lí mǐ tún wéi shì lí mǐ
她的腰围是70**厘米**，臀围是88**厘米**。
Her waist line is 70**cm** and hip line is 88**cm**.

469 离不开 　　　lí bù kāi　　　**Verb:**
　　　　　　　　　　　　　　　　can't do without

bú yào fàng qì wǒ men de jiā lí bù kāi nǐ
不要放弃，我们的家**离不开**你。
Don't give up, our family **cannot do without** you.

470 力气   lì qi   **Noun:** strength (physical)

wǒ fā xiàn nà gè jǔ zhòng yùn dòng yuán de lì qi hěn dà
我 发 现 那 个 举 重 运 动 员 的 **力 气** 很 大。
I noticed that powerlifter had a lot of **strength**.

471 历史   lì shǐ   **Noun:** history

měi gè guó jiā de wén huà hé lì shǐ shì jǐn mì xiāng guān de
每 个 国 家 的 文 化 和 **历 史** 是 紧 密 相 关 的。
Every country's culture and **history** are closely related.

472 立即   lì jí   **Adverb:** immediately

fēi jī liǎng xiǎo shí hòu qǐ fēi wǒ men yào lì jí chū fā
飞 机 两 小 时 后 起 飞，我 们 要 **立 即** 出 发。
The plane takes off in 2 hours and we must set off **immediately**.

473 利息   lì xī   **Noun:** accrual; interest rate

fáng dài lì xī yuè lái yuè gāo mǎi fáng yuè lái yuè nán
房 贷 **利 息** 越 来 越 高，买 房 越 来 越 难。
Mortgage **interest rates** are higher and higher; it's harder and harder to buy a house.

474 利益   lì yì   **Noun:** benefits

xiāng bǐ gǎn qíng tā gèng kàn zhòng lì yì
相 比 感 情，他 更 看 重 **利 益**。
Compared with relationships, he values **benefits** more.

475 俩   liǎ   **Pronoun:** two (people)

suǒ yǐ nǐ men liǎ yǐ hòu zuì hǎo yuǎn lí tā
所 以，你 们 **俩** 以 后 最 好 远 离 他。
So, you **two** better stay away from him in the future.

476 良好　　　　liáng hǎo　　　**Adjective:** good; well (of evaluation)

lǎo shī shuō wǒ ér zi zài xué xiào de biǎo xiàn liáng hǎo
老 师 说 我 儿 子 在 学 校 的 表 现 **良 好** 。
The teacher said my son is performing **well** in school.

477a 量　　　　liáng　　　**Verb:** to measure

jiàn zhù shī míng tiān huì lái liáng fáng zi
建 筑 师 明 天 会 来 量 房 子 。
The architect will come tomorrow **to measure** the house.

477b 量　　　　liàng　　　**Noun:** amount; capacity

zhè shì wèi le jì suàn fān xiū de cái liào yòng liàng
这 是 为 了 计 算 翻 修 的 材 料 用 量 。
This is to calculate the usage **amount** of materials for renovation.

478 粮食　　　　liáng shi　　　**Noun:** foodstuff

tā de gōng sī zuò liáng shi de jìn chū kǒu shēng yi
他 的 公 司 做 **粮 食** 的 进 出 口 生 意 。
His company is doing **foodstuff** import-export business.

479 两边　　　　liǎng biān　　　**Noun:** both sides; each side (of two)

zhè tiáo hé de liǎng biān shì bù tóng de guó jiā
这 条 河 的 **两 边** 是 不 同 的 国 家 。
On each side of the river are two different countries.

480 疗养　　　　liáo yǎng　　　**Verb:** to recuperate; to recover

tā chū yuàn hòu jiù qù le xià wēi yí liáo yǎng
他 出 院 后 ， 就 去 了 夏 威 夷 **疗 养** 。
After he's discharged from the hospital, he went to Hawaii to **recuperate**.

481 了不起　liǎo bu qǐ

Adjective: amazing (due to achievement); great

huā mù lán shì nǚ yīng xióng fēi cháng liǎo bu qǐ
花 木 兰 是 女 英 雄， 非 常 了 不 起!
Hua Mulan was a heroine, very **amazing**!

482 了解　liǎo jiě

Verb: to understand; to know well

wǒ cái rèn shi tā bàn nián bú gòu liǎo jiě tā
我 才 认 识 他 半 年， 不 够 了 解 他。
I've only known him for half a year, so don't **know** him **well** enough.

483 列　liè

Noun: range; line; row

lǎo bǎn ràng wǒ men dà shuǎi mài zhè liè huò pǐn
老 板 让 我 们 大 甩 卖 这 列 货 品。
The boss asked us to put this **line** of goods on big sale.

484 列车　liè chē

Noun: train (generic term)

wǒ měi cì huí lǎo jiā dōu zuò gāo sù liè chē
我 每 次 回 老 家 都 坐 高 速 列 车。
Every time I go back to my hometown, I take high-speed **trains**.

485 列入　liè rù

Verb: to include

jì de bǎ zhè gè liè rù huì yì de yì chéng
记 得 把 这 个 列 入 会 议 的 议 程。
Remember **to include** this on the agenda of the meeting.

486 列为　　　liè wéi　　**Verb:** be classified as; listed as

tā jīn nián bèi fú bù sī liè wéi le shì jiè shǒu fù
他 今 年 被 福 布 斯 列 为 了 世 界 首 富 。
He's **listed as** the world's richest man by Forbes this year.

487 临时　　　lín shí　　**Adjective:** temporary
Adverb: last-minute; temporarily

Adj.
tā zuì jìn quē qián suǒ yǐ zài zuò lín shí gōng zuò
他 最 近 缺 钱 ， 所 以 在 做 临 时 工 作 。
He was short of money recently, so is doing a **temporary** job.

Adv.
wǒ lín shí wàng le dài qián bāo gǎn jué fēi cháng gān gà
我 临 时 忘 了 带 钱 包 ， 感 觉 非 常 尴 尬 。
I forgot to bring my wallet at the **last-minute**, so felt embarrassed.

488 零食　　　líng shí　　**Noun:** snack

wǒ zuì ài de líng shí shì niú nǎi qiǎo kè lì nǐ ne
我 最 爱 的 零 食 是 牛 奶 巧 克 力 ， 你 呢 ？
My favorite **snack** is milk chocolate, how about you?

489 流传　　　liú chuán　　**Verb:** to pass down (time)

tā men de gù shì zài zhōng guó liú chuán le jǐ qiān nián
他 们 的 故 事 在 中 国 流 传 了 几 千 年 。
Their stories have been **passed down** in China for thousands of years.

490 楼梯　　　lóu tī　　**Noun:** stairs; stairway

zāo gāo diàn tī huài le wǒ men zǒu lóu tī ba
糟 糕 ！ 电 梯 坏 了 ， 我 们 走 楼 梯 吧 。
Terrible! The elevator is broken, let's walk the **stairs**.

491 陆地   lù dì   **Noun:** land

dì tú shàng yǒu lù dì dǎo yǔ hé hǎi yáng
地 图 上 有 **陆 地** 、 岛 屿 和 海 洋 。
The map has **land**, islands and ocean.

492 陆续   lù xù   **Adverb:**
one after another

duō shù de guān zhòng yǐ jīng lù xù jìn chǎng le
多 数 的 观 众 已 经 **陆 续** 进 场 了 。
Most of audience entered the arena **one after another**.

493 录取   lù qǔ   **Verb:** to enroll;
be accepted to

tā bèi sī tǎn fú dà xué lù qǔ le zhēn shì hǎo xiāo xi
他 被 斯 坦 福 大 学 **录 取** 了 ! 真 是 好 消 息 。
He got **accepted to** Stanford University! Really good news.

494 律师   lǜ shī   **Noun:** lawyer

sù sòng chéng gōng hòu tā chéng wéi le zhī míng lǜ shī
诉 讼 成 功 后 , 他 成 为 了 知 名 **律 师** 。
Following the successful litigation, he became a renowned **lawyer**.

495 轮   lún   **Verb:** to take turns
(use with other words)

duì wǒ hé tóng shì men lún liú zhí bān
对 , 我 和 同 事 们 **轮** 流 值 班 。
Yes, my colleagues and I **take turns** on duty.

496 轮船   lún chuán   **Noun:** ship

wǒ zài hǎi shàng kàn dào le hěn duō lún chuán hé kuài tǐng
我 在 海 上 看 到 了 很 多 **轮 船** 和 快 艇 。
I saw many **ships** and speedboats on the sea.

497 轮椅　　　lún yǐ　　　**Noun:** wheelchair

zhè xiē lún yǐ shì zhuān mén wèi cán jí rén shè jì de
这 些 **轮 椅** 是 专 门 为 残 疾 人 设 计 的 。
These **wheelchairs** are specially designed for disabled people.

498 轮子　　　lún zi　　　**Noun:** wheel

tiān a lún zi tū rán bào le gāi zěn me bàn
天 啊 ！ **轮 子** 突 然 爆 了 ， 该 怎 么 办 ？
Oh god! The **wheel** suddenly burst, what should I do?

499 论文　　　lùn wén　　　**Noun:** dissertation; thesis

jiào shòu jiàn yì wǒ fā biǎo wǒ de bì yè lùn wén
教 授 建 议 我 发 表 我 的 毕 业 **论 文** 。
The professor suggested that I publish my graduation **thesis**.

500 落　　　luò　　　**Verb:** to fall; to drop

dōng tiān dào le zhè kē shù de yè zi dōu luò le
冬 天 到 了 ， 这 棵 树 的 叶 子 都 **落** 了 。
Winter has arrived, all the leaves of the tree have **fallen**.

501 毛巾　　　máo jīn　　　**Noun:** towel

zhè tiáo máo jīn bù jǐn piào liang ér qiě zhì liàng hěn hǎo
这 条 **毛 巾** 不 仅 漂 亮 ， 而 且 质 量 很 好 。
This **towel** is not only beautiful, but also comes with good quality.

502 毛衣　　　máo yī　　　**Noun:** sweater

wǒ de nán péng yǒu sòng le wǒ yí jiàn lán sè de shèng dàn máo yī
我 的 男 朋 友 送 了 我 一 件 蓝 色 的 圣 诞 **毛 衣** 。
My boyfriend gifted me a blue Christmas **sweater**.

503 帽子　　　mào zi　　　**Noun: hat**

wǒ sòng le tā yì shuāng shǒu tào hé yì dǐng mào zi
我 送 了 他 一 双 手 套 和 一 顶 **帽 子** 。
I gifted him a pair of gloves and a **hat**.

504 没错　　　méi cuò　　　**Phrase: that's right (lit. no mistake)**

méi cuò wǒ men de shèng dàn wǎn cān fēi cháng làng màn
没 错 ！我 们 的 圣 诞 晚 餐 非 常 浪 漫 。
That's right! Our Christmas dinner was very romantic.

505 没法　　　méi fǎ　　　**Phrase: cannot; no way**

wǒ méi fǎ wàng jì tā gěi wǒ jiǎng de xiào huà tài gǎo
我 **没 法** 忘 记 他 给 我 讲 的 笑 话 ， 太 搞
xiào le
笑 了 ！
I **can't** forget the joke he told me, it was so funny!

506 没想到　　　méi xiǎng dào　　　**Phrase: didn't expect**

hā ha méi xiǎng dào tā shì zhè me yōu mò de rén
哈 哈 ， **没 想 到** 他 是 这 么 幽 默 的 人 ！
Haha, I **didn't expect** him to be such a humorous person!

507 美金　　　měi jīn　　　**Noun: dollar (USD)**

zhè tái píng guǒ bǐ jì běn diàn nǎo huā le wǒ bā bǎi měi jīn
这 台 苹 果 笔 记 本 电 脑 花 了 我 八 百 **美 金** 。
This MacBook (Apple laptop) cost me eight hundred **dollars**.

508 美女　　　　měi nǚ　　　**Noun:** beauty; beautiful woman; friendly term to address a young woman

hěn duō hǎo lái wù míng xīng dōu shì shuài gē hé měi nǚ
很 多 好 莱 坞 明 星 都 是 帅 哥 和 **美 女**。
Many Hollywood stars are handsome guys and **beautiful women**.

měi nǚ　qǐng wèn dì tiě zhàn zěn me zǒu
美 女，请 问 地 铁 站 怎 么 走？
Young lady, how can I get to the subway station?

509 梦　　　　mèng　　　**Noun:** dream

zài zuó wǎn de mèng lǐ　wǒ biàn chéng le zhī zhū xiá
在 昨 晚 的 **梦** 里，我 变 成 了 蜘 蛛 侠！
In my **dream** last night, I became Spiderman!

510 梦见　　　　mèng jiàn　　　**Verb:** to dream about

wǒ mèng jiàn zì jǐ gēn yì qún huài dàn dǎ jià
我 **梦 见** 自 己 跟 一 群 坏 蛋 打 架。
I **dreamt** that I was fighting with a bunch of jerks.

511 梦想　　　　mèng xiǎng　　　**Noun:** dream (goals)

huán yóu shì jiè yì zhí shì wǒ de mèng xiǎng
环 游 世 界 一 直 是 我 的 **梦 想**。
Traveling around the world has always been my **dream**.

512 秘密　　　　mì mì　　　**Noun:** secret

qǐng dá yìng wǒ bú yào gào sù bié rén zhè gè mì mì
请 答 应 我，不 要 告 诉 别 人 这 个 **秘 密**。
Please promise me not to tell this **secret** to others.

513 秘书　　　mì shū　　　**Noun:** secretary

tīng shuō, lǎo bǎn hé tā de mì shū yǒu hūn wài qíng
听 说，老 板 和 他 的 **秘书** 有 婚 外 情。
I heard that the boss has an extramarital affair with his **secretary**.

514 密　　　mì　　　**Adjective:** thick; dense

zhè fú huà de tú àn tài mì, wǒ bù xǐ huān
这 幅 画 的 图 案 太 **密**， 我 不 喜 欢。
The pattern of this painting is too **dense**, I don't like it.

515 密码　　　mì mǎ　　　**Noun:** password

zhēn fán, wǒ děi chóng xīn shè zhì yóu xiāng mì mǎ
真 烦，我 得 重 新 设 置 邮 箱 **密码**。
That's annoying, I have to reset my email **password**.

516 密切　　　mì qiè　　　**Adjective:** close (of connection)

zhōng guó hé měi guó yǒu mì qiè de mào yì guān xi
中 国 和 美 国 有 **密切** 的 贸 易 关 系。
China and the United States have **close** trade relations.

517 免费　　　miǎn fèi　　　**Adjective:** free of charge

zhè xiē tián pǐn dōu miǎn fèi, qǐng dà jiā màn yòng
这 些 甜 品 都 **免费**， 请 大 家 慢 用。
These desserts are all **free of charge**, may you all enjoy.

518 面临　　　miàn lín　　　**Verb:** to face (situation)

xīn wén shàng shuō tā men miàn lín yán zhòng de jīng jì wēi jī
新 闻 上 说 他 们 **面临** 严 重 的 经 济 危 机。
The news says they are **facing** a serious economic crisis.

519 面试　　miàn shì

Verb: to interview (job and applications)
Noun: interview

Verb

zǒng jīng lǐ yí gòng dǎ suàn miàn shì jǐ gè rén
总 经 理 一 共 打 算 面 试 几 个 人 ？
How many people does the CEO plan **to interview** in total?

Noun

qǐng nǐ ān pái miàn shì de shí jiān hé dì diǎn
请 你 安 排 面 试 的 时 间 和 地 点 。
Please arrange the time and place of the **interview**.

---

520 描述　　miáo shù

Verb: to describe
Noun: description

Verb

qǐng miáo shù yi xià nǐ wèi lái de wǔ nián guī huà
请 描 述 一 下 你 未 来 的 五 年 规 划 。
Please **describe** your plan for the next five years.

Noun

xiè xie nǐ de miáo shù zhè tīng shàng qù hěn yǒu qù
谢 谢 你 的 描 述 ， 这 听 上 去 很 有 趣 ！
Thanks for the **description**, it sounds interesting!

---

521 描写　　miáo xiě

Verb: to describe (written); to portray

zhè gè gù shì miáo xiě le yí gè zhěng jiù shì jiè de yīng xióng
这 个 故 事 描 写 了 一 个 拯 救 世 界 的 英 雄 。
This story **portrays** a hero who saves the world.

---

522 名牌　　míng pái

Noun: brand name (reputable/famous)

wǒ jué de méi bì yào mǎi míng pái yī fu
我 觉 得 没 必 要 买 名 牌 衣 服 。
I don't think it's necessary to buy **brand name** clothing.

---

523 名片　　míng piàn

Noun: name card; business card

wǒ gāng gāng dé dào le nà wèi dǎo yǎn de míng piàn
我 刚 刚 得 到 了 那 位 导 演 的 名 片 。
I just got that film director's **business card**.

524 名人　　　　　míng rén　　　　**Noun:** celebrity; famous person

^{tā} ^{shì} ^{hǎo} ^{lái} ^{wù} ^{de} ^{míng} ^{rén} ^{yǒu} ^{qián} ^{yǒu} ^{shì}
他 是 好 莱 坞 的 **名 人**， 有 钱 有 势 ！
He's a **celebrity** in Hollywood, rich and powerful!

525 摸　　　　　mō　　　　**Verb:** to touch; to stroke

^{wǒ} ^{xǐ} ^{huān} ^{mō} ^{wǒ} ^{de} ^{gǒu} ^{tā} ^{de} ^{máo} ^{hěn} ^{ruǎn}
我 喜 欢 **摸** 我 的 狗， 它 的 毛 很 软 。
I like **to stroke** my dog, its fur is very soft.

526 模特　　　　　mó tè　　　　**Noun:** model (human)

^{shén} ^{me} ^{zhè} ^{gè} ^{mó} ^{tè} ^{gōng} ^{kāi} ^{pāi} ^{mài} ^{tā} ^{de} ^{chū} ^{yè}
什 么 ！这 个 **模 特** 公 开 拍 卖 她 的 初 夜 ？
What! This **model** publicly auctioned off her first night (viriginity)?

527 模型　　　　　mó xíng　　　　**Noun:** model (machine)

^{wǒ} ^{gěi} ^{wǒ} ^{ér} ^{zi} ^{mǎi} ^{le} ^{yí} ^{gè} ^{fēi} ^{jī} ^{mó} ^{xíng}
我 给 我 儿 子 买 了 一 个 飞 机 **模 型** 。
I bought an airplane **model** for my son.

528 末　　　　　mò　　　　**Noun:** end; last

^{nǐ} ^{kàn} ^{zhè} ^{shì} ^{gōng} ^{sī} ^{de} ^{nián} ^{mò} ^{zǒng} ^{jié} ^{bào} ^{gào}
你 看， 这 是 公 司 的 年 **末** 总 结 报 告 。
You see, this is the company's **end**-of-year summary report.

529 默默　　　　　mò mò　　　　**Adverb:** silently; wholeheartedly

^{zhè} ^{xiē} ^{nián} ^{wǒ} ^{de} ^{lǎo} ^{gōng} ^{yì} ^{zhí} ^{zài} ^{mò} ^{mò} ^{zhī} ^{chí} ^{wǒ}
这 些 年， 我 的 老 公 一 直 在 **默 默** 支 持 我 。
Over the years, my husband has been supporting me **wholeheartedly**.

530 哪怕　　　　nǎ pà　　　　**Conjunction:** even if

哪 怕 我 失 败， 他 也 会 鼓 励 我。
nǎ pà wǒ shī bài tā yě huì gǔ lì wǒ
Even if I fail, he would encourage me.

531 哪　　　　nǎ　　　　which; where

我 忘 了 他 的 生 日 是 哪 天。
wǒ wàng le tā de shēng rì shì nǎ tiān
I forget **which** day is his birthday.

532 男女　　　　nán nǚ　　　　**Noun:** men and women; male and female

这 部 电 影，**男 女** 老 少 都 喜 欢！
zhè bù diàn yǐng nán nǚ lǎo shào dōu xǐ huān
This movie is loved by **men and women**, old and young!

533 男士　　　　nán shì　　　　**Noun:** male figure; man (respectful)

她 的 前 夫 是 商 业 界 的 知 名 **男 士**。
tā de qián fū shì shāng yè jiè de zhī míng nán shì
Her ex-husband was a well-known **figure** in the business world.

534 难免　　　　nán miǎn　　　　**Adjective:** inevitable; unavoidable; **Adverb:** inevitably; unavoidably

Adj.
不 管 是 谁， 犯 错 都 是 **难 免** 的。
bù guǎn shì shéi fàn cuò dōu shì nán miǎn de
No matter who you are, making mistakes is **unavoidable**.

Adv.
他 太 有 钱，**难 免** 在 女 性 中 很 受 欢 迎。
tā tài yǒu qián nán miǎn zài nǚ xìng zhōng hěn shòu huān yíng
He is too rich, **inevitably** very popular among ladies.

535 脑袋 nǎo dai

Noun: head (colloquial)

wǒ zhēn bù dǒng tā de nǎo dai dào dǐ zài xiǎng shén me
我真不懂他的**脑袋**到底在想什么。
I really don't understand what on earth his **head** is thinking.

536 闹 nào

Verb: to fight; to make a noise
Adjective: noisy

Verb
wǒ zài dǎ diàn huà ne ràng hái zi bié nào
我在打电话呢，让孩子别**闹**！
I'm on the phone, ask the child not to **make noises**!

Adj.
jiā lǐ tài nào wǒ bù néng zhuān xīn gōng zuò
家里太**闹**，我不能专心工作。
It's too **noisy** at home, and I can't concentrate on work.

537 闹钟 nào zhōng

Noun: alarm clock

wǒ de nào zhōng měi tiān zǎo shàng liù diǎn bàn jiào xǐng wǒ
我的**闹钟**每天早上六点半叫醒我。
My **alarm clock** wakes me up at 6:30 every morning.

538 内部 nèi bù

Noun: interior; internal

yǒu shí hòu nèi bù máo dùn bǐ wài bù máo dùn fù zá
有时候，**内部**矛盾比外部矛盾复杂。
Sometimes **internal** conflicts are more complex than external ones.

539 内科 nèi kē

Noun: internal medicine

tā shì nèi kē yī shēng wǒ shì wài kē yī shēng
她是**内科**医生，我是外科医生。
She's a physician (**internal medicine** doctor) and I'm a surgeon.

540 能干   néng gàn   **Adjective:** capable

tā yòu cōng míng yòu néng gàn hěn kuài jiù shēng zhí le
她 又 聪 明 又 **能 干**, 很 快 就 升 职 了 !
She's smart and **capable**, so got promoted quickly!

541 宁静   níng jìng   **Adjective:** peaceful; tranquil

zhè lǐ de huán jìng hěn ān jìng ràng wǒ de xīn hěn níng jìng
这 里 的 环 境 很 安 静, 让 我 的 心 很 **宁 静**。
The environment here is quiet; it makes my heart **peaceful**.

542 浓   nóng   **Adjective:** strong; concentrated

zhè bēi kā fēi de wèi dào hěn nóng nà bēi de yǒu diǎn dàn
这 杯 咖 啡 的 味 道 很 **浓**, 那 杯 的 有 点 淡。
This cup of coffee's taste is **strong**, that cup's is a bit weak.

wǒ yì bān huà dàn zhuāng bù huà nóng zhuāng
我 一 般 化 淡 妆, 不 化 **浓 妆**。
I usually wear light makeup, not **heavy** makeup.

543 女士   nǚ shì   **Noun:** Ma'am; lady

nǚ shì men xiān shēng men qǐng jǔ bēi qìng zhù
女 士 们, 先 生 们, 请 举 杯 庆 祝 !
Ladies and gentlemen, raise your glasses to celebrate!

544 暖气   nuǎn qì   **Noun:** heating; heater

wǒ yào zài xīn jiā ān zhuāng kōng tiáo hé nuǎn qì
我 要 在 新 家 安 装 空 调 和 **暖 气**。
I want to install air conditioning and **heating** in my new home.

545 拍照　pāi zhào　**Verb:** take a picture/photograph

qǐng wèn nǐ kě yǐ bāng wǒ men pāi zhào ma
请 问，你 可 以 帮 我 们 **拍 照** 吗？
Excuse me, can you **take a photo** for us?

546 排列　pái liè　**Verb:** to line up; to arrange

xué shēng men zài cāo chǎng shàng pái liè zuò yùn dòng
学 生 们 在 操 场 上 **排 列** 做 运 动。
Students are **lining up** to play sports on the playground.

547 牌　pái　**Noun:** brand; cards

tā shì gè dǔ guǐ tiān tiān qù dǔ chǎng dǎ pái
他 是 个 赌 鬼，天 天 去 赌 场 打 **牌**。
He is a gambler who goes to the casino to play **cards** daily.

548 盘　pán　**Classifier** for tray, dish, plate of food

jīn wǎn wǒ gěi kè rén men zuò le yì pán gōng bǎo jī dīng
今 晚 我 给 客 人 们 做 了 一 **盘** 宫 保 鸡 丁。
Tonight I made a **plate** of Kung Pao Chicken for the guests.

549 盘子　pán zi　**Noun:** plate

zhè tào pán zi fēi cháng jīng měi shì zài nǎ lǐ mǎi de
这 套 **盘 子** 非 常 精 美！是 在 哪 里 买 的？
This **plate** set is gorgeous! Where did you buy it?

550 胖子　pàng zi　**Noun:** fat person

tā xiǎo de shí hòu shì gè shòu zi xiàn zài shì gè pàng zi
他 小 的 时 候 是 个 瘦 子，现 在 是 个 **胖 子**。
He was a thin kid when he was young, and now he is a **fat person**.

551 培训   péi xùn

Verb: to train
Noun: training

Verb

jīng lǐ ràng wǒ fù zé péi xùn xīn yuán gōng
经 理 让 我 负 责 培 训 新 员 工 。
The manager put me in charge of **training** new employees.

Noun

zhè cì de péi xùn shì yí gè bàn yuè
这 次 的 培 训 是 一 个 半 月 。
This **training** lasts for one and a half months.

552 培训班   péi xùn bān   **Noun:** training class

wǒ de shuāng bāo tāi nǚ ér zài shàng xī bān yá yǔ péi xùn bān
我 的 双 胞 胎 女 儿 在 上 西 班 牙 语 培 训 班 。
My twin girls are taking Spanish **training classes**.

553 培养   péi yǎng

Verb: to foster;
to develop

péi yǎng hǎo de xué xí xí guàn fēi cháng zhòng yào
培 养 好 的 学 习 习 惯 非 常 重 要 。
It is very important **to develop** good study habits.

554 培育   péi yù

Verb: to cultivate;
to educate

niú jīn dà xué péi yù le hěn duō chū míng de zhèng kè
牛 津 大 学 培 育 了 很 多 出 名 的 政 客 。
Oxford University has **cultivated** many famous politicians.

555 批   pī

Classifier for goods
or groups (a batch of;
bunch of)

zhè pī huà zhuāng pǐn shì cóng hán guó jìn kǒu de
这 批 化 妆 品 是 从 韩 国 进 口 的 。
This **batch of** cosmetics was imported from South Korea.

556 批   pī

Verb: to mark; to correct; to criticize (use with other words)

lǎo shī zài bàn gōng shì pī xué shēng de zuò yè
老师在办公室批学生的作业。
The teacher is **marking** the students' homework in the office.

lǎo shī pī píng le zhāng wén dàn shì biǎo yáng le wáng míng
老师批评了张文，但是表扬了王明。
The teacher **criticized** Zhang Wen, but praised Wang Ming.

557 片面   piàn miàn

Adjective: one-sided

wǒ jué de tā duì zhè jiàn shì de píng jià hěn piàn miàn
我觉得他对这件事的评价很片面。
I think his judgement of this matter is very **one-sided**.

558 品质   pǐn zhì

Noun: quality (of product)

zhè xiē chǎn pǐn méi yǒu dá dào wǒ men de pǐn zhì biāo zhǔn
这些产品没有达到我们的品质标准。
These products did not meet our **quality** standards.

559 平方   píng fāng

Noun: square (use with measurement)

wǒ de gōng yù dà gài shì jiǔ shí píng fāng mǐ
我的公寓大概是九十平方米。
My apartment is about ninety **square** meters.

560 平静   píng jìng

Adjective: calm; peaceful

zhè shǒu gē ràng wǒ men de xīn qíng hěn píng jìng
这首歌让我们的心情很平静。
This song makes our mood very **peaceful**.

561 平均   píng jūn   **Adjective:** average

nǐ men guó jiā de píng jūn gōng zī shì duō shǎo
你 们 国 家 的 **平 均** 工 资 是 多 少 ？
What is the **average** salary in your country?

562 平稳   píng wěn   **Adjective:** smooth; steady

tā jīng yàn fēng fù kāi chē kāi de hěn píng wěn
他 经 验 丰 富， 开 车 开 得 很 **平 稳**。
He is experienced and drives very **smoothly**.

563 迫切   pò qiè   **Adjective:** urgent; pressing
                                              Adverb: urgently

Adj.
bìng rén de qíng kuàng pò qiè jiā rén men hěn dān xīn
病 人 的 情 况 **迫 切**， 家 人 们 很 担 心。
The patient's condition is **urgent**; the family members are worried.

Adv.
tā shī xuè guò duō xiàn zài pò qiè xū yào shū xuè
他 失 血 过 多， 现 在 **迫 切** 需 要 输 血。
He lost a lot of blood; now **urgently** need blood transfusion.

564 破产   pò chǎn   **Verb:** to bankrupt
                                              Noun: bankruptcy

Verb
lǎo bǎn gāng gāng pò chǎn le gōng sī yě dǎo bì le
老 板 刚 刚 **破 产** 了， 公 司 也 倒 闭 了。
The boss just went **bankrupt** and his company closed down too.

Noun
hěn kě xī tā de pò chǎn shì bù kě bì miǎn de
很 可 惜， 他 的 **破 产** 是 不 可 避 免 的。
Unfortunately, his **bankruptcy** was inevitable.

565 妻子   qī zi   **Noun:** wife (formal term)

zhàng fu hé qī zi yīng gāi yì qǐ fēn dān jiā wù
丈 夫 和 **妻 子** 应 该 一 起 分 担 家 务。
Husband and **wife** should share housework together.

566 期待   qī dài   **Verb:** to expect; look forward to

wǒ qī dài huí zhōng guó kàn jiā rén hé péng yǒu
我 **期 待** 回 中 国 看 家 人 和 朋 友。
I **look forward to** returning to China to see family and friends.

567 期间   qī jiān   **Noun:** period (of time)

zài shàng hǎi qī jiān   wǒ men yì qǐ qù le dí shì ní
在 上 海 **期 间**, 我 们 一 起 去 了 迪 士 尼
lè yuán
乐 园。
During our **period** in Shanghai, we went to Disneyland together.

568 期末   qī mò   **Noun:** end of term

qī mò kǎo shì kuài dào le   wǒ de yā lì hěn dà
期 末 考 试 快 到 了, 我 的 压 力 很 大。
End of term exams are approaching; I'm under a lot of pressure.

569 期限   qī xiàn   **Noun:** time limit; deadline

qǐng wèn kě yǐ yán cháng zhè gè xiàng mù de qī xiàn ma
请 问, 可 以 延 长 这 个 项 目 的 **期 限** 吗?
Excuse me, can we extend the **deadline** of this project?

570 期中   qī zhōng   **Noun:** midterm

lǐng dǎo men zài nǔ lì zhǔn bèi qī zhōng de xuǎn jǔ
领 导 们 在 努 力 准 备 **期 中** 的 选 举。
Leaders are working hard to prepare for the **midterm** elections.

571 其余　qí yú　**Pronoun:** the rest

wǒ men dǎ sǎo wèi shēng, qí yú rén zhuāng bàn shèng dàn shù
我 们 打 扫 卫 生，**其 余** 人 装 扮 圣 诞 树 。
Let's clean up, while **the rest** decorate the Christmas tree.

572 企业　qǐ yè　**Noun:** enterprise

tā shì qǐ yè jiā, mèng xiǎng shì jiàn lì zì jǐ de qǐ yè
他 是 企 业 家，梦 想 是 建 立 自 己 的 **企 业** 。
He is an entrepreneur who dreams to build his own **enterprise**.

573 气球　qì qiú　**Noun:** balloon

wǒ mǎi le hěn duō wǔ yán liù sè de shēng rì qì qiú
我 买 了 很 多 五 颜 六 色 的 生 日 **气 球** 。
I bought a lot of colorful birthday **balloons**.

574 汽水　qì shuǐ　**Noun:** soft drink

wǒ diǎn le yì píng qì shuǐ, tā diǎn le yì bēi lù chá
我 点 了 一 瓶 **汽 水**，他 点 了 一 杯 绿 茶 。
I ordered a bottle of **soft drink**; he ordered a cup of green tea.

575 汽油　qì yóu　**Noun:** gasoline

zuì jìn wù jià shàng zhǎng, qì yóu zhǎng jià le
最 近 物 价 上 涨，**汽 油** 涨 价 了 。
There's inflation recently, and the price of **gasoline** has increased.

576 器官　qì guān　**Noun:** organ

bìng rén fǎn duì zuò qì guān de qiē chú shǒu shù
病 人 反 对 做 **器 官** 的 切 除 手 术 。
The patient objected to the **organ** removal surgery.

577 前头　qián tou　**Noun:** front; thereinbefore

yī yuàn de qián tóu shì tíng chē chǎng　hòu tou shì gōng yuán
医 院 的 **前 头** 是 停 车 场 ，后 头 是 公 园 。
The **front** of the hospital is a car park and the back is a public park.

578 前途　qián tú　**Noun:** future prospect

tā yòu cōng míng yòu néng gàn　shì yè qián tú hěn hǎo
他 又 聪 明 又 能 干 ，事 业 **前 途** 很 好 ！
He is smart and capable, and has good **future** career **prospects**!

579 浅　qiǎn　**Adjective:** shallow

zhè biān de hé shuǐ hěn qiǎn　nà biān de hěn shēn
这 边 的 河 水 很 **浅** ， 那 边 的 很 深 。
The river water on this side is **shallow**, on that side it's deep.

580 巧克力　qiǎo kè lì　**Noun:** chocolate

wǒ hěn ài chī niú nǎi qiǎo kè lì　nǐ ne
我 很 爱 吃 牛 奶 **巧 克 力** ， 你 呢 ？
I love eating milk **chocolate**, how about you?

581 切　qiē　**Verb:** to cut

má fán nǐ bāng wǒ bǎ tǔ dòu qiē chéng tiáo
麻 烦 你 帮 我 把 土 豆 **切** 成 条 。
May I trouble you **to cut** the potatoes into strips for me.

582 亲爱　qīn ài　**Adjective:** dear

tā shì wǒ de lǎo tóng xué　yě shì wǒ qīn ài de péng yǒu
他 是 我 的 老 同 学 ，也 是 我 **亲 爱** 的 朋 友 。
He is my old classmate and my **dear** friend.

583 亲密 qīn mì **Adjective:** close; intimate (relationship)

wǔ nián lái wǒ men de guān xi yì zhí hěn qīn mì
五 年 来 我 们 的 关 系 一 直 很 **亲 密**。
In the past 5 years, our relationship has always been **close**.

584 青春 qīng chūn **Noun:** youth

qīng chūn shì měi gè rén zuì bǎo guì de cái fù
青 春 是 每 个 人 最 宝 贵 的 财 富。
Youth is everyone's most precious wealth.

585 轻松 qīng sōng **Adjective:** relaxed; relaxing

yì biān kàn shū yì biān tīng yīn yuè hěn qīng sōng
一 边 看 书， 一 边 听 音 乐 很 **轻 松**。
Reading a book while listening to music is very **relaxing**.

586 轻易 qīng yì **Adverb:** easily; rashly

hǎo hǎo sī kǎo bú yào qīng yì xià jié lùn
好 好 思 考， 不 要 **轻 易** 下 结 论。
Have a good think about it, and don't come to conclusions **rashly**.

587 清醒 qīng xǐng **Adjective:** sober; clear-headed

tā hē zuì le bù tài qīng xǐng suǒ yǐ shuō hú huà
他 喝 醉 了， 不 太 **清 醒**， 所 以 说 胡 话。
He was drunk and not very **clear-headed**, so talked nonsense.

588 情景 qíng jǐng **Noun:** scene; circumstance

wǒ yǒng yuǎn dōu bú huì wàng jì tā fā fēng de qíng jǐng
我 永 远 都 不 会 忘 记 他 发 疯 的 **情 景**。
I will never forget the **scene** of him going mad.

589 穷   qióng   **Adjective:** poor (no money)

_{tā} _{céng} _{jīng} _{hěn} _{yǒu} _{qián}   _{kě} _{shì} _{xiàn} _{zài} _{yǒu} _{diǎn} _{qióng}
他 曾 经 很 有 钱 ， 可 是 现 在 有 点 **穷** 。
He used to be rich, but now he is a little **poor**.

590 穷人   qióng rén   **Noun:** poor people; the poor

_{tā} _{fēn} _{bié} _{jīng} _{lì} _{le} _{fù} _{rén} _{hé} _{qióng} _{rén} _{de} _{shēng} _{huó}
他 分 别 经 历 了 富 人 和 **穷 人** 的 生 活 。
He experienced the lives of the rich and **the poor** respectively.

591 秋季   qiū jì   **Noun:** autumn; fall (season)

_{tā} _{men} _{zài} _{qiū} _{jì} _{dìng} _{hūn}   _{zài} _{chūn} _{jì} _{jié} _{hūn}
他 们 在 **秋 季** 订 婚 ， 在 春 季 结 婚 。
They got engaged in the **fall** and married in the spring.

592 趋势   qū shì   **Noun:** trend; tendency

_{wǒ} _{dān} _{xīn} _{fáng} _{dài} _{lì} _{xī} _{yǒu} _{shàng} _{zhǎng} _{de} _{qū} _{shì}
我 担 心 房 贷 利 息 有 上 涨 的 **趋 势** 。
I am worried that there is a **trend** of rising interest rates on mortgages.

593 圈   quān   **Noun:** circle

_{wǒ} _{de} _{péng} _{yǒu} _{quān} _{yǒu} _{yì} _{xiē} _{qū} _{yán} _{fù} _{shì} _{de} _{rén}
我 的 朋 友 **圈** 有 一 些 趋 炎 附 势 的 人 。
There are some opportunistic people in my **circle** of friends.

594 权利   quán lì   **Noun:** right

_{méi} _{yǒu} _{rén} _{kě} _{yǐ} _{qīn} _{fàn} _{wǒ} _{de} _{fǎ} _{lù} _{quán} _{lì}
没 有 人 可 以 侵 犯 我 的 法 律 **权 利** 。
No one can violate my legal **rights**.

595 却   què   **Adverb:** but; yet

tā xìng gé nèi xiàng què dài rén fēi cháng rè qíng
他 性 格 内 向 **却** 待 人 非 常 热 情 。
He is introverted in personality **but** treats people very warmly.

596 确认   què rèn   **Verb:** to confirm

qǐng què rèn yi xià nǐ de chū shēng rì qī hé dì zhǐ
请 **确 认** 一 下 你 的 出 生 日 期 和 地 址 。
Please quickly **confirm** your date of birth and address.

597 然而   rán ér   **Conjunction:** however

wǒ yǐ wéi tā zhēn de ài wǒ rán ér fā xiàn shì jiǎ de
我 以 为 他 真 的 爱 我 ，**然 而** 发 现 是 假 的 。
I thought he truly loved me, **however** discovered it was fake.

598 燃料   rán liào   **Noun:** fuel

qǐng què bǎo fēi jī yǒu zú gòu de rán liào
请 确 保 飞 机 有 足 够 的 **燃 料** 。
Please ensure that the plane has enough **fuel**.

599 (燃)烧   rán shāo   **Verb:** to burn

nà chǎng dà huǒ rán shāo de tài kuài hěn nán kòng zhì
那 场 大 火 **燃 烧** 得 太 快 ， 很 难 控 制 。
That big fire **burned** so fast it was hard to control.

600 热闹   rè nao   **Adjective:** bustling; lively (environment)

tā xǐ huān rè nao de dì fang tǎo yàn lěng qīng de dì fang
她 喜 欢 **热 闹** 的 地 方 ， 讨 厌 冷 清 的 地 方 。
She likes **lively** places and hates deserted places.

601 热心   rè xīn   **Adjective:** enthusiastic; warm-hearted

zhè gè nǚ fú wù yuán duì gù kè fēi cháng rè xīn
这 个 女 服 务 员 对 顾 客 非 常 **热 心** 。
This waitress is very **enthusiastic** toward customers.

602 人家   rén jiā   **Noun:** household
Pronoun: the other person (colloquial)

Noun
zhè gè shān gǔ zhǐ yǒu èr shí hù rén jiā
这 个 山 谷 只 有 二 十 户 **人 家** 。
There are only twenty **households** in this valley.

Pro.
rú guǒ nǐ bù shuō rén jiā zěn me zhī dào nǐ xǐ huān tā
如 果 你 不 说 ，**人 家** 怎 么 知 道 你 喜 欢 她 ？
If you don't say it, how would **the other person** know that you like her?

603 日记   rì jì   **Noun:** diary

wǒ cóng lái méi yǒu xiě rì jì de xí guàn nǐ ne
我 从 来 没 有 写 **日 记** 的 习 惯 ， 你 呢 ？
I never have the habit of writing a **diary**, how about you?

604 日历   rì lì   **Noun:** calendar

wǒ de péng yǒu sòng le wǒ yì běn zhōng yīng wén rì lì
我 的 朋 友 送 了 我 一 本 中 英 文 **日 历** 。
My friend gifted me a Chinese and English **calendar**.

605 如今   rú jīn   **Noun:** nowadays

rú jīn huì shuō zhōng wén de wài guó péng yǒu yuè lái yuè duō
如 今 会 说 中 文 的 外 国 朋 友 越 来 越 多 。
Nowadays more and more foreign friends can speak Chinese.

606 弱　　　ruò　　　**Adjective:** weak

tā gāng gāng chū yuàn　shēn tǐ hái yǒu diǎn ruò
她 刚 刚 出 院， 身 体 还 有 点 弱 。
She's just been discharged from the hospital and is still a bit **weak**.

607 伞　　　sǎn　　　**Noun:** umbrella

wǒ mǎi le yí fù tài yáng jìng hé yì bǎ sǎn
我 买 了 一 副 太 阳 镜 和 一 把 伞 。
I bought a pair of sunglasses and an **umbrella**.

608a 散　　　sǎn　　　**Adjective:** loose; dispersed

wǒ qù chāo shì mǎi le yì xiē sǎn zhuāng de jiān guǒ
我 去 超 市 买 了 一 些 散 装 的 坚 果 。
I went to the supermarket to buy some **loose** packed nuts.

608b 散　　　sàn　　　**Verb:** to scatter; to disseminate

bì yè hòu tóng xué men sàn zài le quán guó gè dì
毕 业 后， 同 学 们 散 在 了 全 国 各 地 。
After graduation, my classmates were **scattered** all over the country.

609 扫　　　sǎo　　　**Verb:** to sweep

wǒ sǎo shù yè tā bāng wǒ dào lā jī
我 扫 树 叶， 他 帮 我 倒 垃 圾 。
I **swept** the leaves, and he helped me take out the trash.

610 色   sè

Noun: color;
look/expression
(use with other words)

wǒ hěn xǐ huān qiǎn lán sè hé shēn hóng sè
我 很 喜 欢 浅 蓝 色 和 深 红 色 。
I really like light blue (**color**) and dark red (**color**).

wǒ zhǐ shì hěn mí huò bié gěi wǒ nà yàng de yǎn sè
我 只 是 很 迷 惑， 别 给 我 那 样 的 眼 色 。
I'm just very confused, don't give me that kind of **look**.

611 色彩   sè cǎi   **Noun:** color

zhè jiān shū fáng de sè cǎi hé fēng gé hěn dā pèi
这 间 书 房 的 色 彩 和 风 格 很 搭 配 。
The **color** and style of this study room are well coordinated.

612 森林   sēn lín   **Noun:** forest

tā jiā nóng chǎng de hòu miàn shì yí piàn dà sēn lín
他 家 农 场 的 后 面 是 一 片 大 森 林 。
Behind his family's farm is a big **forest**.

613 晒   shài

Verb: to post/display
(publically);
to dry in the sun

tā cháng cháng zài shè jiāo méi tǐ shàng shài lǚ yóu zhào piàn
她 常 常 在 社 交 媒 体 上 晒 旅 游 照 片 。
She often **posts** travel photos on social media.

wǒ xiǎng bǎ bèi zi hé zhěn tou ná chū qù shài
我 想 把 被 子 和 枕 头 拿 出 去 晒 。
I want to take out the quilt and pillow **to dry in the sun**.

614 闪   shǎn

Verb: to dodge;
to flash; to shine

wǒ gāng gāng kàn dào wǒ qián nán yǒu cóng mén kǒu shǎn guò
我 刚 刚 看 到 我 前 男 友 从 门 口 闪 过 。
I just saw my ex-boyfriend **dodge** away by the door.

615 闪电　　shǎn diàn　　**Noun:** lightning

wǒ cóng xiǎo jiù hěn hài pà dǎ léi hé shǎn diàn
我 从 小 就 很 害 怕 打 雷 和 闪 电 。
I've been terrified of thunder and **lightning** since I was a child.

616 善良　　shàn liáng　　**Adjective:** virtuous; kind-hearted

suī rán tā cóng qián hěn xié è dàn xiàn zài hěn shàn liáng
虽 然 他 从 前 很 邪 恶 ， 但 现 在 很 善 良 。
Although he was evil before, he is **kind-hearted** now.

617 善于　　shàn yú　　**Verb:** be good at

tā shàn yú tán jí tā wǒ shàn yú tán gāng qín
他 善 于 弹 吉 他 ， 我 善 于 弹 钢 琴 。
He is **good at** playing guitar and I am **good at** playing piano.

618 伤害　　shāng hài　　**Verb:** to hurt
Noun: damage

Verb
wǒ men yào bǎo hù hái zi fáng zhǐ huài rén shāng hài tā men
我 们 要 保 护 孩 子 ， 防 止 坏 人 伤 害 他 们 。
We need to protect the kids and prevent bad people from **hurting** them.

Noun
yǒu xiē xīn lǐ shāng hài shì hěn nán zhì yù de
有 些 心 理 伤 害 是 很 难 治 愈 的 。
Some psychological **damage** is difficult to heal.

619 商务　　shāng wù　　**Noun:** commerce; business affairs

wǒ de qián nǚ yǒu duì diàn zǐ shāng wù fēi cháng gǎn xìng qù
我 的 前 女 友 对 电 子 商 务 非 常 感 兴 趣 。
My ex-girlfriend was very interested in e-**commerce**.

620 赏

shǎng

Verb: to award; to appreciate

huáng dì hěn gāo xìng， shǎng le yì hé jīn zi gěi tā

皇 帝 很 高 兴，赏 了 一 盒 金 子 给 他。

The emperor was happy and **awarded** him a box of gold.

621 上个月

shàng gè yuè

Noun: last month

wǒ shàng gè yuè qù le měi guó， xià gè yuè yào qù yīng guó

我 上 个 月 去 了 美 国，下 个 月 要 去 英 国。

I went to the US **last month** and will go to the UK next month.

622 上楼

shàng lóu

Verb: to go upstairs

kuài shàng lóu， tā zài lóu shàng děng nǐ hěn jiǔ le

快 上 楼，她 在 楼 上 等 你 很 久 了。

Go upstairs quickly, she's been waiting for you upstairs for a long time.

623 上门

shàng mén

Verb: drop in; door-to-door

tā de gōng sī wèi gù kè tí gōng shàng mén fú wù

他 的 公 司 为 顾 客 提 供 上 门 服 务。

His company provides **door-to-door** service for customers.

624 烧

shāo

Verb: to burn; to cook (colloquial)

wǒ mā yí gè rén zài chú fáng shāo fàn， wǒ qù bāng tā

我 妈 一 个 人 在 厨 房 烧 饭，我 去 帮 她。

My mom is **cooking** in the kitchen alone, I'm going to help her.

625 设施

shè shī

Noun: facilities

wǒ men gōng sī de kē jì shè shī fēi cháng xiān jìn

我 们 公 司 的 科 技 设 施 非 常 先 进。

Our company's technological **facilities** are very advanced.

626 设置　　　shè zhì　　**Verb:** to set up
　　　　　　　　　　　　　Noun: setting

Verb
qǐng nǐ bāng wǒ shè zhì zhè tái xīn diàn nǎo
请 你 帮 我 设 置 这 台 新 电 脑 。
Please help me **to set up** this new computer.

Noun
wǒ xū yào gēng xīn wǒ de shǒu jī shè zhì
我 需 要 更 新 我 的 手 机 设 置 。
I need to update my phone **settings**.

627 申请　　　shēn qǐng　　**Verb:** to apply
　　　　　　　　　　　　　Noun: application

Verb
wǒ xū yào shēn qǐng zhōng guó de lǚ yóu qiān zhèng
我 需 要 申 请 中 国 的 旅 游 签 证 。
I need **to apply** for a Chinese tourist visa.

Noun
nǐ kě yǐ zài guān fāng wǎng zhàn shàng tián shēn qǐng biǎo gé
你 可 以 在 官 方 网 站 上 填 申 请 表 格 。
You can fill out the **application** form on the official website.

628 身材　　　shēn cái　　**Noun:** body figure

tā tiān tiān zuò yú jiā shēn cái yuè lái yuè hǎo
她 天 天 做 瑜 伽 ， 身 材 越 来 越 好 。
She does yoga every day, and her **figure** gets better and better.

629 身份　　　shēn fèn　　**Noun:** identity

xiǎo xīn yǒu xiē kǒng bù fèn zǐ gù yì yǐn cáng shēn fèn
小 心 ， 有 些 恐 怖 分 子 故 意 隐 藏 身 份 。
Be careful, some terrorists deliberately hide their **identities**.

630 身高　　　shēn gāo　　**Noun:** height

tā shēn gāo yì mǐ qī wǔ tǐ zhòng qī shí gōng jīn
他 身 高 一 米 七 五 ， 体 重 七 十 公 斤 。
His **height** is 1.75 meters and his weight is 70 kilograms.

631 深厚 shēn hòu **Adjective:** deep; profound; solid

guò qù shí nián, wǒ men jiàn lì le shēn hòu de yǒu yì
过 去 十 年 ， 我 们 建 立 了 深 厚 的 友 谊 。
Over the past ten years, we have established a **profound** friendship.

632 神话 shén huà **Noun:** myth

nǐ tīng shuō guò 《cháng é bēn yuè》 de shén huà gù shì ma
你 听 说 过 《嫦 娥 奔 月》 的 神 话 故 事 吗 ？
Have you heard the **myth** of "Chang'e Flying to the Moon"?

633 神秘 shén mì **Adjective:** mysterious

duì wǒ men lái shuō, zǒng cái shì gè shén mì rén wù
对 我 们 来 说 ， 总 裁 是 个 神 秘 人 物 。
To us, the CEO is a **mysterious** figure.

634 甚至 shèn zhì **Conjunction:** even

wǒ men shén zhì bù zhī dào tā de hūn yīn zhuàng kuàng
我 们 甚 至 不 知 道 他 的 婚 姻 状 况 。
We don't **even** know his marital status.

635 失败 shī bài **Verb:** to fail
Noun: failure

Verb
suī rán wǒ men shàng cì shī bài le, dàn zhè cì chéng gōng le
虽 然 我 们 上 次 失 败 了 ， 但 这 次 成 功 了 。
Although we **failed** last time, we succeeded this time.

Noun
yào jì zhù： shī bài shì chéng gōng zhī mǔ
要 记 住 ： 失 败 是 成 功 之 母 。
Remember: **failure** is the mother of success.

636 失望　shī wàng　Adjective: disappointed

tīng shuō tā yào cí zhí　zǒng jiān hěn shī wàng
听 说 他 要 辞 职 ， 总 监 很 **失 望** 。
Hearing that he's going to resign, the director was **disappointed**.

637 失业　shī yè　Verb: to lose job / Noun: unemployment

Verb
gōng sī dǎo bì hòu　suǒ yǒu de yuán gōng dōu shī yè le
公 司 倒 闭 后 ， 所 有 的 员 工 都 **失 业** 了 。
After the company closed down, all employees **lost their jobs**.

Noun
xīn wén shàng shuō shī yè rén shù zài yì qiān rén zuǒ yòu
新 闻 上 说 **失 业** 人 数 在 一 千 人 左 右 。
The news said that the **unemployment** figure (unemployed people) is around 1,000.

638 诗　shī　Noun: poetry; poem

tā nián qīng de shí hòu hěn làng màn　xǐ huān xiě ài qíng shī
他 年 轻 的 时 候 很 浪 漫 ， 喜 欢 写 爱 情 **诗** 。
He was romantic when he was young and liked writing love **poems**.

639 诗人　shī rén　Noun: poet

dāng shí　tā shì wén xué jiè yǒu míng de shī rén
当 时 ， 他 是 文 学 界 有 名 的 **诗 人** 。
At that time, he was a well-known **poet** in the literary world.

640 湿　shī　Adjective: damp; humid; wet

zhēn qí guài　tā de shàng yī shì gān de　kù zi què
真 奇 怪 ， 他 的 上 衣 是 干 的 ， 裤 子 却
shì shī de
是 **湿** 的 。
So strange, his top is dry but his trousers are **wet**.

641 实施　　shí shī

Verb: to implement
Noun: implementation

Verb

rén shì bù mén dǎ suàn shí shī xīn de zhāo pìn fāng àn
人 事 部 门 打 算 **实 施** 新 的 招 聘 方 案 。

The HR department plans **to implement** a new recruitment scheme.

Noun

wáng zǒng fù zé jù tǐ fāng àn de shí shī
王 总 负 责 具 体 方 案 的 **实 施** 。

Director Wang is responsible for the **implementation** of the specific scheme.

642 实用　　shí yòng

Adjective: practical

wǒ men hái xū yào zhì dìng shí yòng de jì huà
我 们 还 需 要 制 订 **实 用** 的 计 划 。

We also need to formulate **practical** plans.

643 食堂　　shí táng

Noun: canteen; dining room

tài bàng le dà xué de shí táng yǒu zhōng cān yě yǒu
太 棒 了 ！大 学 的 **食 堂** 有 中 餐 ， 也 有
xī cān
西 餐 。

Great! The university's **canteen** serves both Chinese and Western food.

644 使劲　　shǐ jìn

Verb: to strive hard (physically); exert all one's strength

dà jiā shǐ jìn wǒ men yí dìng yào yíng zhè chǎng bá hé
大 家 **使 劲**! 我 们 一 定 要 赢 这 场 拔 河
bǐ sài
比 赛 。

Strive hard everyone! We must win this tug of war.

645 士兵   shì bīng   **Noun:** soldiers

qí shí hěn duō shì bīng tǎo yàn zhàn zhēng rè ài hé píng
其 实 ， 很 多 **士 兵** 讨 厌 战 争 ， 热 爱 和 平 。
In fact, many **soldiers** hate war and love peace.

646 市区   shì qū   **Noun:** downtown; urban area

tā zài shì qū yǒu yí tào gōng yù zài jiāo qū yǒu yí
他 在 **市 区** 有 一 套 公 寓 ， 在 郊 区 有 一
tào fáng zi
套 房 子 。
He has an apartment **downtown** and a house in the suburbs.

647 似的   shì de   **Auxiliary:** like; as if (indicate similarity)

tā tiào wǔ de yàng zi xiàng gè xiǎo chǒu shì de
他 跳 舞 的 样 子 像 个 小 丑 **似 的** 。
The appearance of him dancing is **like** that of a clown.

648 事物   shì wù   **Noun:** thing; matter

tā xǐ huān mào xiǎn zǒng shì duì xīn xiān shì wù yǒu xìng qù
她 喜 欢 冒 险 ， 总 是 对 新 鲜 **事 物** 有 兴 趣 。
She loves adventure and is always interested in new **things**.

649 事先   shì xiān   **Adverb:** prior; in advance

rú guǒ nǐ lái wǒ jiā yào shì xiān tōng zhī wǒ
如 果 你 来 我 家 ， 要 **事 先** 通 知 我 。
If you come to my house, let me know **in advance**.

650 试卷　　shì juàn　　**Noun:** exam paper

lǐ lǎo shī zài jiào xué lóu pī gǎi shì juàn
李 老 师 在 教 学 楼 批 改 **试 卷** 。
Teacher Li is marking the **exam papers** in the teaching building.

651 是否　　shì fǒu　　**Adverb:** whether or not

wǒ xiǎng zhī dào tā shì fǒu zhēn xīn ài wǒ
我 想 知 道 他 **是 否** 真 心 爱 我 。
I want to know **whether** he truly loves me **or not**.

652 收回　　shōu huí　　**Verb:** to withdraw; to take back

kǒng pà tā hěn kuài huì shōu huí zhè xiē tóu zī
恐 怕 他 很 快 会 **收 回** 这 些 投 资 。
I'm afraid he will **withdraw** these investments soon.

653 收获　　shōu huò　　**Verb:** to gain; to obtain
Noun: good results; gains

Verb
zhè cì chū chāi ràng wǒ shōu huò le hěn duō rén mài
这 次 出 差 让 我 **收 获** 了 很 多 人 脉 。
This business trip allowed me to **gain** a lot of contacts.

Noun
gēn tā men jiàn lì hé zuò guān xi shì zuì dà de shōu huò
跟 他 们 建 立 合 作 关 系 是 最 大 的 **收 获** 。
Establishing a partnership with them is the biggest **gain**.

654 收益　　shōu yì　　**Noun:** benefit; profit

lǚ yóu yè gěi dāng dì dài lái le hěn duō jīng jì shōu yì
旅 游 业 给 当 地 带 来 了 很 多 经 济 **收 益** 。
Tourism has brought a lot of economic **benefits** to the local area.

655 手工   shǒu gōng   **Adjectvive:** manual; handmade

zhè tiáo wéi jīn zhì liàng hěn hǎo, shì shǒu gōng de
这 条 围 巾 质 量 很 好， 是 手 工 的。
This scarf is of good quality and is **handmade**.

656 手里   shǒu lǐ   in one's hands

yào shi zài tā de shǒu lǐ, wǒ děi gěi tā dǎ diàn huà
钥 匙 在 他 的 手 里， 我 得 给 他 打 电 话。
The key is **in his hand**, I need to call him.

657 手术   shǒu shù   **Noun:** surgery; operation

yī shēng shuō tā bì xū zuò ái xì bāo de qiē chú shǒu shù
医 生 说 他 必 须 做 癌 细 胞 的 切 除 手 术。
The doctor said he has to do **surgery** for cancer cell removal.

658 手套   shǒu tào   **Noun:** glove

zhè shuāng shǒu tào shì wǒ mā gěi wǒ zhī de, hěn zhēn guì
这 双 手 套 是 我 妈 给 我 织 的， 很 珍 贵！
These **gloves** were knitted by my mother, so very precious!

659 守   shǒu   **Verb:** to guard; to defend

wǒ de gǒu xǐ huān shǒu zài mén kǒu, jiù xiàng gè bǎo ān
我 的 狗 喜 欢 守 在 门 口， 就 像 个 保 安！
My dog likes **to guard** at the door, just like a security guard!

660 首 shǒu

Classifier for songs and poems
Adjective: leading; first

Class.
wǒ gāng gāng xià zǎi le jǐ shǒu zhōng wén liú xíng gē
我 刚 刚 下 载 了 几 **首** 中 文 流 行 歌。
I just downloaded several Chinese pop songs.

Adj.
tā shì shǒu gè zài niǔ yuē shí dài guǎng chǎng biǎo yǎn de yì rén
他 是 **首** 个 在 纽 约 时 代 广 场 表 演 的 艺 人。
He was the **first** artist to perform at New York's Times Square.

661 受不了 shòu bu liǎo

Phrase: had enough; cannot bear

zhè fèn gōng zuò de gōng zī tài dī wǒ shòu bu liǎo
这 份 工 作 的 工 资 太 低！我 **受 不 了**。
The wages for this job are too low! I **can't bear** it.

662 售货员 shòu huò yuán **Noun:** salesperson

wǒ kàn dào yǒu gè gù kè zài hé shòu huò yuán chǎo jià
我 看 到 有 个 顾 客 在 和 **售 货 员** 吵 架。
I saw a customer arguing with the **salesperson**.

663 叔叔 shū shu

Noun: uncle; respectful term to address an older man

wǒ shū shu xiǎo shí hòu cháng cháng hé wǒ bà dǎ jià
我 **叔 叔** 小 时 候 常 常 和 我 爸 打 架。
When my **uncle** was a child, he often fought with my dad.

ér zi duì sī jī shū shu shuō xiè xie
儿 子，对 司 机 **叔 叔** 说 谢 谢。
Son, say thank you to the driver (**uncle**).

664 舒适 shū shì

Adjective: comfortable (physical)

zhè jiàn nèi yī shì sī chóu de chuān zhe hěn shū shì
这 件 内 衣 是 丝 绸 的， 穿 着 很 **舒 适**。
The underwear is made of silk, very **comfortable** to wear.

665 熟练   shú liàn   **Adjective:** proficient/ skilled (through practice)

tā shì xīn shǒu　gōng zuò jì qiǎo hái bú gòu shú liàn
他 是 新 手， 工 作 技 巧 还 不 够 **熟 练** 。

He is a novice, so his work skills are not **proficient** enough.

666 暑假   shǔ jià   **Noun:** summer vacation

xiāng bǐ hán jià　wǒ men gèng qī dài shǔ jià
相 比 寒 假， 我 们 更 期 待 **暑 假** 。

Compared to winter vacation, we look forward to **summer vacation** more.

667 树林   shù lín   **Noun:** woods

tuán duì zài kǎo lǜ yào bu yào zài shù lín lù yíng
团 队 在 考 虑 要 不 要 在 **树 林** 露 营 。

The team is considering whether to camp in the **woods**.

668 树叶   shù yè   **Noun:** tree leaf

wǒ de hái zi ài kàn wǔ yán liù sè de shù yè
我 的 孩 子 爱 看 五 颜 六 色 的 **树 叶** 。

My kids love looking at the colorful **tree leaves**.

669 数据   shù jù   **Noun:** data

tā yì biān kàn bào gào　yì biān fēn xī xiāo shòu shù jù
他 一 边 看 报 告， 一 边 分 析 销 售 **数 据** 。

He is reading the report while analyzing the sales **data**.

670 数码   shù mǎ   **Noun:** digital; code

tā gěi wǒ de lǐ wù shì gè shù mǎ xiàng jī
他 给 我 的 礼 物 是 个 **数 码** 相 机 。

The gift he gave me was a **digital** camera.

671 刷　　shuā　　**Verb:** to brush; to scrub; to paint

wǒ yào qǐng jǐ gè gōng rén bāng wǒ men shuā qiáng
我 要 请 几 个 工 人 帮 我 们 **刷** 墙 。
I'm going to hire some workers to help us **paint** the walls.

672 刷牙　　shuā yá　　**Verb:** brush teeth

yī shēng jiàn yì wǒ yòng diàn zǐ yá shuā shuā yá
医 生 建 议 我 用 电 子 牙 刷 **刷牙** 。
The doctor advised me to **brush** my **teeth** with an electric toothbrush.

673 刷子　　shuā zi　　**Noun:** brush

zhè gè shuā zi tài jiù le wǒ yào qù mǎi gè xīn de
这 个 **刷子** 太 旧 了 ， 我 要 去 买 个 新 的 。
This **brush** is so old, I'm going to buy a new one.

674 帅　　shuài　　**Adjective:** handsome

tā yòu shuài yòu yǒu qián dāng rán shòu huān yíng
他 又 **帅** 又 有 钱 ， 当 然 受 欢 迎 。
He is **handsome** and rich, and of course popular.

675 帅哥　　shuài gē　　**Noun:** handsome guy; friendly term to address a young man

xiǎo xīn nà gè shuài gē shì gè huā huā gōng zǐ
小 心 ， 那 个 **帅哥** 是 个 花 花 公 子 。
Be careful, that **handsome** guy is a playboy.

shuài gē nǐ kě yǐ bāng wǒ men pāi zhào ma
帅哥 ， 你 可 以 帮 我 们 拍 照 吗 ？
Young man, can you take a photo for us?

676 率先　shuài xiān　**Adverb:** to take the lead

yīng gé lán zú qiú duì **shuài xiān** jìn rù bàn jué sài le
英 格 兰 足 球 队 **率 先** 进 入 半 决 赛 了 ！
The England football team **took the lead** to reach the semi-finals!

677 睡着　shuì zháo　**Verb:** to fall asleep

tài hǎo le wǒ de shuāng bāo tāi ér zi zhōng yú dōu **shuì**
太 好 了 ！ 我 的 双 胞 胎 儿 子 终 于 都 **睡**
zháo le
着 了 ！
So good! My twin sons are finally both **falling asleep**!

678 顺序　shùn xù　**Noun:** sequence; order

qǐng àn zhào zhè gè **shùn xù** gěi tā men bān jiǎng
请 按 照 这 个 **顺 序** 给 他 们 颁 奖 。
Please award prizes for them according to this **order**.

679 说不定　shuō bu dìng　**Adverb:** maybe

bié hài xiū **shuō bu dìng** tā yě duì nǐ yǒu hǎo gǎn
别 害 羞 ， **说 不 定** 她 也 对 你 有 好 感 。
Don't be shy, **maybe** she feels for you as well.

680 说服　shuō fú　**Verb:** to persuade

yào bù wǒ **shuō fú** tā gēn nǐ qù kàn diàn yǐng
要 不 ， 我 **说 服** 她 跟 你 去 看 电 影 。
Perhaps, I shall **persuade** her to go to the movies with you.

681 思考   sī kǎo   **Verb:** to think (deeply)
Noun: reflection; thoughts

Verb
tā men xū yào shí jiān sī kǎo shēng yì shī bài de yuán yīn
他 们 需 要 时 间 **思 考** 生 意 失 败 的 原 因。
They need time **to think** about the reason of their business failure.

Noun
bù tóng de rén yǒu bù tóng de sī kǎo fāng shì
不 同 的 人 有 不 同 的 **思 考** 方 式。
Different people have different ways of **thinking**.

682 似乎   sì hū   **Adverb:** seemingly; it seems

sì hū tā men de shāng pǐn méi yǒu zú gòu de jìng zhēng lì
似 乎 他 们 的 商 品 没 有 足 够 的 竞 争 力。
It seems that their product doesn't have sufficient competitiveness.

683 松   sōng   **Adjective:** loose; relax

zhè tiáo duǎn kù tài sōng shè jì de bù hǎo
这 条 短 裤 太 **松**， 设 计 得 不 好！
These shorts are too **loose**, the design is not good!

684 松树   sōng shù   **Noun:** pine tree

sōng shù shàng yǒu jǐ zhī sōng shǔ zài chī sōng guǒ
松 树 上 有 几 只 松 鼠 在 吃 松 果。
There are several squirrels eating pine cones on the **pine tree**.

685 塑料   sù liào   **Noun:** plastic

wǒ men yào xiǎng bàn fǎ jiǎn shǎo sù liào lā jī
我 们 要 想 办 法 减 少 **塑 料** 垃 圾。
We need to find ways to reduce **plastic** waste.

686 塑料袋   sù liào dài   **Noun:** plastic bag

huán bǎo jī gòu gǔ lì dà jiā huí shōu sù liào dài
环 保 机 构 鼓 励 大 家 回 收 **塑 料 袋** 。
Environmental agencies encourage us to recycle **plastic bags**.

687 酸   suān   **Adjective:** sour

níng méng hěn suān hěn duō rén bù xǐ huān zhí jiē chī
柠 檬 很 **酸** ， 很 多 人 不 喜 欢 直 接 吃 。
Lemons are **sour**; many people don't like to eat them straight.

688 酸奶   suān nǎi   **Noun:** yogurt

tā shì sù shí zhǔ yì zhě bù chī suān nǎi děng nǎi zhì pǐn
他 是 素 食 主 义 者 ， 不 吃 **酸 奶** 等 奶 制 品 。
He is vegan and does not eat dairy products such as **yogurt**.

689 随手   suí shǒu   **Adverb:** readily; casually (without thought or planning)

lǎo shī gào sù hái zi bú yào suí shǒu rēng lā jī
老 师 告 诉 孩 子 不 要 **随 手** 扔 垃 圾 。
The teacher told the children not to **causally** throw rubbish (litter).

690 孙女   sūn nǚ   **Noun:** granddaughter

tīng shuō tā de sūn nǚ zài sī lì xué xiào shàng xué
听 说 他 的 **孙 女** 在 私 立 学 校 上 学 。
I heard that his **granddaughter** attends a private school.

691 孙子   sūn zi   **Noun:** grandson

qí guài de shì tā de sūn zi què zài gōng lì xué xiào shàng xué
奇 怪 的 是 ， 他 的 **孙 子** 却 在 公 立 学 校 上 学 。
Surprisingly, his **grandson** actually goes to a state school.

692 缩短   suō duǎn   **Verb:** to shorten

他 把 项 目 期 限 从 一 个 月 **缩 短** 到 了 两
个 周 。

He **shortened** the project deadline from one month to two weeks.

693 缩小   suō xiǎo   **Verb:** to narrow; shrink; zoom out

电 脑 屏 幕 有 放 大 和 **缩 小** 的 功 能 。

A computer screen has the ability to zoom in and **zoom out**.

694 台阶   tái jiē   **Noun:** steps

我 看 到 他 一 个 人 坐 在 **台 阶** 上 抽 烟 。

I saw him sitting on the **steps** smoking a cigarette by himself.

695 台上   tái shàng   on stage; on the platform

有 句 谚 语 : **台 上** 一 分 钟 , 台 下 十 年 功 !

There is a proverb: one minute **on stage**, ten years off stage!

696 躺   tǎng   **Verb:** to lie (down)

我 好 累 , 只 想 **躺** 在 沙 发 上 休 息 一 下 。

I'm so tired, just want **to lie** on the sofa to have a rest.

697 套餐　　　　tào cān　　　**Noun:** set (of food or service)

huǒ guō de tào cān jià gé shì sān bǎi yuán bú tài guì
火锅的**套餐**价格是三百元，不太贵。
The **set** price of the hot pot is 300 yuan, not too expensive.

698 特价　　　　tè jià　　　**Noun:** special offer; bargain price

zhè shì dǎ zhé hòu de tè jià yuán jià shì wǔ bǎi yuán
这是打折后的**特价**，原价是五百元。
This is a discounted **special price**, the original price is 500 yuan.

699 特殊　　　　tè shū　　　**Adjective:** special; privileged

guó jiā de lǐng dǎo rén yǒu nǎ xiē tè shū de dài yù
国家的领导人有哪些**特殊**的待遇？
What **special** treatment do the leaders of the country have?

700 特征　　　　tè zhēng　　　**Noun:** feature

zhěng xíng shǒu shù gǎi biàn le tā de liǎn bù tè zhēng
整形手术改变了他的脸部**特征**。
Plastic surgery changed his facial **features**.

701 提供　　　　tí gōng　　　**Verb:** to provide

zhèng fǔ wèi nàn mín tí gōng le shí wù hé zhù sù
政府为难民**提供**了食物和住宿。
The government **provided** food and accommodation for the refugees.

702 提醒   tí xǐng   **Verb:** to remind
Noun: reminder

Verb
qǐng fā yóu jiàn tí xǐng kè hù jí shí fù kuǎn
请 发 邮 件 提 醒 客 户 及 时 付 款 。
Please send an email **to remind** clients to pay promptly.

Noun
tài hǎo le xiè xie nǐ de tí xǐng
太 好 了 ！ 谢 谢 你 的 提 醒 ！
Very good! Thanks for your **reminder**!

703 体操   tǐ cāo   **Noun:** gymnastics

yǒu xiē xué shēng zài cāo chǎng shàng zuò tǐ cāo
有 些 学 生 在 操 场 上 做 体 操 。
Some students are doing **gymnastics** on the playground.

704 体检   tǐ jiǎn   **Noun:** physical examination

wǒ bà qù yī yuàn zuò dìng qī tǐ jiǎn le
我 爸 去 医 院 做 定 期 体 检 了 。
My dad went to the hospital for his regular **physical examination**.

705 体重   tǐ zhòng   **Noun:** body weight

yī shēng shuō bǎo chí shēn gāo hé tǐ zhòng de píng héng
医 生 说 保 持 身 高 和 体 重 的 平 衡
hěn zhòng yào
很 重 要 。
Doctors say it's important to maintain a balance of height and **weight**.

706 替   tì   **Verb:** for (on behalf of); take the place of;

qǐng nǐ tì wǒ xiàng nǐ de xiōng dì jiě mèi wèn hǎo
请 你 替 我 向 你 的 兄 弟 姐 妹 问 好 。
Please say hello to your brothers and sisters **for** me.

707 替代　　tì dài　　**Verb:** to replace; to substitute

tā cí zhí le　　lǎo bǎn zài zhǎo rén tì dài tā
他 辞 职 了， 老 板 在 找 人 替 代 他。
He resigned and the boss is looking for someone to **replace** him.

708 天真　　tiān zhēn　　**Adjective:** naïve

zhè gè xià shǔ tài tiān zhēn　　bèi tā de shàng sī piàn le
这 个 下 属 太 天 真， 被 他 的 上 司 骗 了。
This subordinate is so **naïve**, he was deceived by his superior.

709 填　　tián　　**Verb:** to fill (out); to write

qǐng xiān tián biǎo　　rán hòu qiān zì
请 先 填 表， 然 后 签 字。
Please **fill out** the form first and then sign it.

710 填空　　tián kòng　　**Verb:** to fill in the blanks

zhè dào tí xū yào wǒ men yòng zhè xiē cí huì tián kòng
这 道 题 需 要 我 们 用 这 些 词 汇 填 空。
This question requires us to **fill in the blanks** with these vocabulary.

711 挑　　tiāo　　**Verb:** to pick　**Adjective:** picky

Verb
wǒ men yào qù shèng dàn shì chǎng tiāo lǐ wù
我 们 要 去 圣 诞 市 场 挑 礼 物。
We're going to the Christmas market **to pick out** presents.

Adj.
zài fàn shí fāng miàn　　wǒ ér zi hěn tiāo
在 饭 食 方 面， 我 儿 子 很 挑。
My son is very **picky** when it comes to meals.

712 挑选   tiāo xuǎn   **Verb:** to choose; to select

wǒ gěi lǎo gōng tiāo xuǎn le yí kuài ruì shì míng biǎo
我 给 老 公 挑 选 了 一 块 瑞 士 名 表。
I **chose** a famous Swiss watch for my husband.

713 调皮   tiáo pí   **Adjective:** naughty

wǒ de gǒu jiù xiàng wǒ de hái zi, yòu kě ài yòu tiáo pí
我 的 狗 就 像 我 的 孩 子， 又 可 爱 又 调 皮！
My dog is like my child, cute and **naughty**!

714 挑   tiǎo   **Verb:** to hold up; to raise

nǐ kàn dào le ma? tā zài duì nǐ tiǎo méi
你 看 到 了 吗？ 她 在 对 你 挑 眉。
Did you see it? She was **raising** her eyebrow at you.

715 挑战   tiǎo zhàn   **Verb:** to challenge / **Noun:** challenge

Verb
zài zhè cì bǐ sài, měi guó duì huì tiǎo zhàn bā xī duì
在 这 次 比 赛， 美 国 队 会 挑 战 巴 西 队。
In this competition, the US team will **challenge** the Brazilian team.

Noun
jiā yóu! bié fàng qì, wǒ men yí dìng huì kè fú tiǎo zhàn
加 油！ 别 放 弃， 我 们 一 定 会 克 服 挑 战。
Come on! Don't give up, we will definitely overcome the **challenges**.

716 贴   tiē   **Verb:** to stick; to paste; to glue

qǐng bāng wǒ bǎ biāo qiān tiē zài bāo zhuāng zhǐ shàng
请 帮 我 把 标 签 贴 在 包 装 纸 上。
Please help me **to stick** the label on the wrapping paper.

717 停下   tíng xià   **Verb:** to stop

^{sī jī shī fu} ^{qǐng nǐ zài qián miàn de lù kǒu tíng xià}
司 机 师 傅 ， 请 你 在 前 面 的 路 口 停 下 。
Master driver, please **stop** at the intersection ahead.

718 挺   tǐng   **Verb:** to stand out; to keep; to puff out
Adverb: very, quite

Verb
^{pāi zhào de shí hòu} ^{yào tǐng xiōng shōu fù}
拍 照 的 时 候 ， 要 挺 胸 收 腹 ！
When taking photos, **puff out** your chest and belly in!

Adv.
^{tā shì tǐng nǔ lì de} ^{dà jiā dōu xīn shǎng tā}
她 是 挺 努 力 的 ， 大 家 都 欣 赏 她 。
She is indeed **quite** hardworking, everyone appreciates her.

719 通知书   tōng zhī shū   **Noun:** notice letter (formal notice paper)

^{wǒ gāng gāng shōu dào le dà xué lù qǔ tōng zhī shū}
我 刚 刚 收 到 了 大 学 录 取 通 知 书 。
I just received my college acceptance **notice letter**.

720 同情   tóng qíng   **Verb:** to sympathize
Noun: sympathy

Verb
^{tā tóng qíng nà gè qǐ gài gěi tā mǎi le yì bēi kā fēi}
他 同 情 那 个 乞 丐 ， 给 他 买 了 一 杯 咖 啡 。
He **sympathized** with the beggar and bought him a cup of coffee.

Noun
^{wǒ zài tā shēn shàng kàn dào le tóng qíng hé shàn liáng}
我 在 他 身 上 看 到 了 同 情 和 善 良 。
I see **sympathy** and kindness in him.

721 童话   tóng huà   **Noun:** fairy tale

^{wǒ xiǎo de shí hòu xǐ huān shōu jí tóng huà shū}
我 小 的 时 候 喜 欢 收 集 童 话 书 。
When I was little, I loved collecting **fairy tale** books.

722 童年　　　　tóng nián　　　**Noun:** childhood; babyhood

wǒ de tóng nián shì zài xiāng xià dù guò de
我 的 **童 年** 是 在 乡 下 度 过 的 。
My **childhood** was spent in the countryside.

723 统计　　　　tǒng jì　　　　**Verb:** to add up; to count; to compile statistics

wǒ gāng gāng tǒng jì le， péi xùn bān yí gòng yǒu gè
我 刚 刚 **统 计** 了， 培 训 班 一 共 有 56 个
xué shēng
学 生 。
I just **counted**, there are 56 students in the training class.

724 统一　　　　tǒng yī　　　　**Verb:** to unify (formal)

gōng yuán qián 221 nián， qín shǐ huáng tǒng yī le zhōng guó
公 元 前 221 年， 秦 始 皇 **统 一** 了 中 国 。
In 221 BC, Emperor Qin Shihuang **unified** China.

725 痛快　　　　tòng kuài　　　**Adjective:** joyous; delightful

tā men yì biān hē jiǔ yì biān chàng gē， fēi cháng tòng kuài
他 们 一 边 喝 酒 一 边 唱 歌， 非 常 **痛 快** ！
They sang while drinking, so **joyous**!

726 投　　　　tóu　　　　**Verb:** to cast; to throw

qǐng bāng wǒ bǎ zhè fēng xìn tóu jìn xìn xiāng
请 帮 我 把 这 封 信 **投** 进 信 箱 。
Please **cast** this letter into the mailbox for me.

727 投入　tóu rù　**Verb:** to put into

tā wèi xīn gōng sī **tóu rù** le hěn duō shí jiān hé jīng lì
他 为 新 公 司 **投 入** 了 很 多 时 间 和 精 力。
He **put** a lot of time and energy **into** the new company.

728 投诉　tóu sù　**Verb:** to sue; to make a complaint (formal)　**Noun:** complaint

Verb
zhè gè guān yuán yīn wèi huì lù bèi **tóu sù** le
这 个 官 员 因 为 贿 赂 被 **投 诉** 了。
The official was **sued** for bribery.

Noun
gōng zuò rén yuán zhèng zài chǔ lǐ tā men de **tóu sù**
工 作 人 员 正 在 处 理 他 们 的 **投 诉**。
Staff are processing their **complaints**.

729 投资　tóu zī　**Verb:** to invest　**Noun:** investment

Verb
jīn nián tā zài fáng dì chǎn háng yè **tóu zī** le yì qiān wàn
今 年 他 在 房 地 产 行 业 **投 资** 了 一 千 万
měi yuán
美 元。
This year he **invested** $10 million into the real estate industry.

Noun
wǒ duì lǐ cái hé **tóu zī** dōu fēi cháng gǎn xìng qù
我 对 理 财 和 **投 资** 都 非 常 感 兴 趣。
I am very interested in both financial management and **investment**.

730 透　tòu　**Verb:** to pass through; to leak; to appear　**Adverb:** extremely

Verb
tā gāng gāng xiàng wǒ **tòu** le tā men qiāo qiāo dìng hūn de xiāo xi
他 刚 刚 向 我 **透** 了 他 们 悄 悄 订 婚 的 消 息。
He just **leaked** the news of their secret engagement to me.

Adv.
fēn shǒu hòu tā de qián nǚ yǒu hèn **tòu** le tā
分 手 后, 他 的 前 女 友 恨 **透** 了 他。
After the breakup, his ex-girlfriend hated him **extremely**.

731 透(明)　　tòu míng　　**Adjective:** transparent; see-through

zhè tiáo qún zi yǒu diǎn tòu míng bú tài shì hé chuān
这 条 裙 子 有 点 **透 明** ，不 太 适 合 穿 。
The skirt is a bit **transparent**, not very suitable to wear.

732 图案　　tú àn　　**Noun:** pattern; image design

nǐ xǐ huān zhōng shì qīng huā cí de tú àn ma
你 喜 欢 中 式 青 花 瓷 的 **图 案** 吗 ？
Do you like the **pattern** of Chinese blue and white porcelain?

733 途中　　tú zhōng　　on the way to; en route

tā zài huí jiā de tú zhōng yù dào qiǎng jié fàn le
她 在 回 家 的 **途 中** 遇 到 抢 劫 犯 了 。
She encountered a robber **on her way** home.

734 土地　　tǔ dì　　**Noun:** land

zhè kuài tǔ dì de miàn jī dà gài shì shí gōng qīng
这 块 **土 地** 的 面 积 大 概 是 十 公 顷 。
This area of the **land** is about ten hectares.

735 推迟　　tuī chí　　**Verb:** to delay; to postpone

yīn wèi dǔ chē wǒ bù dé bù tuī chí kāi huì shí jiān
因 为 堵 车 ，我 不 得 不 **推 迟** 开 会 时 间 。
Due to the traffic jam, I had **to postpone** the meeting time.

736 推销　　tuī xiāo　　**Verb:** to promote (sales)

xīn zǒng jiān fù zé tuī xiāo chǎn pǐn dào yà zhōu shì chǎng
新 总 监 负 责 **推 销** 产 品 到 亚 洲 市 场 。
The new director is in charge of **promoting** the product to Asian market.

737 脱   tuō   **Verb:** to take off; to undress

wǒ nǚ ér sān suì jiù néng zì jǐ chuān yī fu hé tuō
我 女 儿 三 岁 就 能 自 己 穿 衣 服 和 **脱**
yī fu
衣 服 。

My daughter has been able to dress and **undress** herself since the age of 3.

738 袜子   wà zi   **Noun:** socks

wǒ mǎi le yì shuāng báo tuǐ wà hé liǎng shuāng hòu wà zi
我 买 了 一 双 薄 腿 袜 和 两 双 厚 **袜 子** 。

I bought one pair of thin leg stockings and two pairs of thick **socks**.

739 外汇   wài huì   **Noun:** foreign exchange; foreign currency

wǒ yǒu yí gè lǎo péng yǒu cóng shì wài huì jiāo yì
我 有 一 个 老 朋 友 从 事 **外 汇** 交 易 。

I have an old friend who does **foreign exchange** trading.

740 外交官   wài jiāo guān   **Noun:** diplomat

tā de yí gè qīn qi shì yí wèi gāo jí wài jiāo guān
他 的 一 个 亲 戚 是 一 位 高 级 **外 交 官** 。

One of his relatives is a senior **diplomat**.

741 外套   wài tào   **Noun:** coat

wǒ dìng zuò le yí tào xī zhuāng hé liǎng jiàn wài tào
我 定 做 了 一 套 西 装 和 两 件 **外 套** 。

I have a suit and two **coats** made for myself.

742 弯   wān   **Adjective:** curly; bend; crooked

yǐ qián tā de tóu fā yǒu diǎn wān xiàn zài hěn zhí
以 前 他 的 头 发 有 点 弯 ， 现 在 很 直 。
His hair used to be a little **curly**, but now it's straight.

743 晚点   wǎn diǎn   **Adjective:** late; behind schedule

zāo gāo fēi jī huì wǎn diǎn sān gè bàn xiǎo shí
糟 糕 ！飞 机 会 晚 点 三 个 半 小 时 。
Terrible! The plane will be three and a half hours **late**.

744 万一   wàn yī   **Conjunction:** in case

wàn yī tā bù xǐ huān zhè gè lǐ wù jiù gěi tā hóng bāo
万 一 他 不 喜 欢 这 个 礼 物 ，就 给 他 红 包 。
In case he doesn't like the gift, give him a red packet.

745 王   wáng   **Noun:** monarch (use with other words)

ōu zhōu yǒu xiē guó jiā réng rán bǎo liú guó wáng hé nǚ wáng
欧 洲 有 些 国 家 仍 然 保 留 国 王 和 女 王 。
Some countries in Europe still retain **kings** and **queens**.

746 网络   wǎng luò   **Noun:** network

xiàn zài wǎng luò tài kǎ bù néng kàn shì pín
现 在 网 络 太 卡 ， 不 能 看 视 频 。
The **network** is so stuck now, I can't watch videos.

747 网址   wǎng zhǐ   **Noun:** internet site; website; URL

qǐng gào sù wǒ xià zǎi miǎn fèi tú piàn de wǎng zhǐ
请 告 诉 我 下 载 免 费 图 片 的 网 址 。
Please tell me the **URL** to download free pictures.

748 微笑   wēi xiào   **Verb:** to smile
Noun: smile

Verb

yì kāi shǐ， tā zhǐ shì wēi xiào， rán hòu què tū rán
一 开 始， 她 只 是 **微 笑，** 然 后 却 突 然
dà xiào
大 笑 ！

At first, she just **smiled**, then suddenly burst out laughing!

Noun

wǒ bèi tā de wēi xiào mí zhù le
我 被 她 的 **微 笑** 迷 住 了 ！

I'm mesmerized by her **smile**!

749 微信   wēi xìn   **Noun:** WeChat
(Chinese social app)

wǒ gāng gāng yòng wēi xìn gěi tā zhuǎn le sì bǎi yuán
我 刚 刚 用 **微 信** 给 他 转 了 四 百 元。

I just transferred 400 yuan to him via **WeChat**.

750 围巾   wéi jīn   **Noun:** scarf

tā gěi wǒ de shēng rì lǐ wù shì yì tiáo hóng wéi jīn
她 给 我 的 生 日 礼 物 是 一 条 红 **围 巾** 。

Her birthday present to me is a red **scarf**.

751 维持   wéi chí   **Verb:** to maintain

wéi chí hé zuò guān xi duì shuāng fāng dōu hěn zhòng yào
维 持 合 作 关 系 对 双 方 都 很 重 要。

Maintaining the partnership is important to both sides.

752 维护   wéi hù   **Verb:** to uphold

nǐ yào dǒng de wéi hù zì jǐ de fǎ lǜ quán lì
你 要 懂 得 **维 护** 自 己 的 法 律 权 利。

You need to know how to **uphold** your legal rights.

753 维修 — wéi xiū — **Verb:** to repair (machine)

wǒ de diàn shì jī huài le , xū yào wéi xiū
我 的 电 视 机 坏 了 , 需 要 维 修 。
My TV is broken and needs **to be repaired**.

754 尾巴 — wěi ba — **Noun:** tail

rú guǒ gǒu duì nǐ yáo wěi ba , shuō míng tā xǐ huān nǐ
如 果 狗 对 你 摇 尾 巴 , 说 明 它 喜 欢 你 。
If a dog wags its **tail** at you, it means it likes you.

755 未必 — wèi bì — **Adverb:** not necessarily

duì yú xīn shǒu , zuò shēng yì wèi bì huì chéng gōng
对 于 新 手 , 做 生 意 未 必 会 成 功 。
For beginners, doing business will **not necessarily** be successful.

756 未来 — wèi lái — **Noun:** far future

yě xǔ zài wèi lái huǒ xīng huì shì hé rén lèi jū zhù
也 许 在 未 来 火 星 会 适 合 人 类 居 住 。
Perhaps in the (**far**) **future** Mars will be suitable for human habitation.

757 位于 — wèi yú — **Verb:** to be located in

wǒ men de xīn gōng yù wèi yú shì zhōng xīn
我 们 的 新 公 寓 位 于 市 中 心 。
Our new apartment is **located** in the city center.

758 位置 — wèi zhì — **Noun:** position; location

guān yú mǎi fáng , wèi zhì shì zuì zhòng yào de
关 于 买 房 , 位 置 是 最 重 要 的 。
When it comes to buying a house, **location** is most important.

759 味(儿)　　wèi'r　　**Noun:** taste; flavor (food, smell, metaphorical sense)

zhè shì shén me wèi 'r yǒu diǎn chòu
这 是 什 么 味 儿 ， 有 点 臭 ！
What is this **smell**, it a bit stinky!

760a 喂　　wèi　　**Verb:** to feed

wǒ yào yòng jīn tiān mǎi de gǒu liáng wèi gǒu
我 要 用 今 天 买 的 狗 粮 喂 狗 。
I'm going **to feed** the dog with the dog food I bought today.

760b 喂　　wéi　　**Greeting:** hi; hello (for phone calls)

wéi wǒ shì zhāng fēi qǐng wèn nín shì nǎ wèi
喂 ！ 我 是 张 飞 ， 请 问 您 是 哪 位 ？
Hello! I'm Zhang Fei, who I am speaking to?

761 稳　　wěn　　**Adjective:** still; steady

qǐng nǐ zuò wěn wǒ yào kāi mó tuō chē le
请 你 坐 稳 ， 我 要 开 摩 托 车 了 ！
Please sit **still**, I'm going to drive the motorcycle!

762 稳定　　wěn dìng　　**Adjective:** stable

dà xué bì yè hòu tā zhǎo le yí fèn wěn dìng de gōng zuò
大 学 毕 业 后 ， 她 找 了 一 份 稳 定 的 工 作 。
After graduating from university, she found a **stable** job.

763 问候　　wèn hòu　　**Verb:** to greet

qǐng nǐ dài wǒ xiàng nǐ de yé ye nǎi nai wèn hòu
请 你 代 我 向 你 的 爷 爷 奶 奶 问 候 。
Please **greet** your paternal grandparents on my behalf.

764 无 — wú — **Verb:** not; without

fù mǔ xiǎng bāng tā mǎi fáng, ràng tā wú jīng jì fù dān
父母想帮他买房，让他**无**经济负担。

His parents want to help him buy a house to allow him to be **without** a financial burden.

765 无法 — wú fǎ — **Adverb:** unable

tā men zhǐ néng fù shǒu fù, wú fǎ fù quán kuǎn
他们只能付首付，**无法**付全款。

They can only make a down payment, **unable** to make the full amount.

766 无聊 — wú liáo — **Adjective:** boring

zhè gè huà tí yǒu diǎn wú liáo, shuō gè yǒu qù de ba
这个话题有点**无聊**，说个有趣的吧。

This topic is a bit **boring**, let's talk about something interesting.

767 无论 — wú lùn — **Conjunction:** no matter

wú lùn tā yǒu qián méi qián, wǒ dōu huì ài tā
无论他有钱没钱，我都会爱他。

No matter he has money or not, I will always love him.

768 无数 — wú shù — **Adjective:** countless

tā fēi cháng shuài! dāng rán yǒu wú shù nǚ fěn sī
他非常帅！当然有**无数**女粉丝。

He is very handsome! Of course he has **countless** female fans.

769 无所谓 — wú suǒ wèi — **Phrase:** don't mind

jīn wǎn chī shén me dōu kě yǐ, wǒ wú suǒ wèi
今晚吃什么都可以，我**无所谓**。

I can eat anything tonight, I **don't mind**.

770 无限   wú xiàn   **Adjective:** infinite; unlimited

wǒ de shǒu jī nèi cún shì yǒu xiàn de bù shì wú xiàn de
我 的 手 机 内 存 是 有 限 的 , 不 是 无 限 的 。
My phone memory is limited, not **unlimited**.

771 五颜六色   wǔ yán liù sè   **Idiom:** colorful; multicolored

wǒ shōu jí le hěn duō wǔ yán liù sè de shù yè
我 收 集 了 很 多 五 颜 六 色 的 树 叶 。
I've collected many **colorful** leaves.

772 误会   wù huì   **Verb:** to misunderstand / **Noun:** misunderstanding

Verb

bié shēng qì nǐ kě néng wù huì tā de huà le
别 生 气 , 你 可 能 误 会 他 的 话 了 。
Don't be angry, you may have **misunderstood** his words.

Noun

wǒ xī wàng nǐ men néng kuài diǎn jiě chú wù huì
我 希 望 你 们 能 快 点 解 除 误 会 。
I hope you can clear up the **misunderstanding** soon.

773 西瓜   xī guā   **Noun:** watermelon

zhè lǐ yǒu dōng guā huáng guā xī guā hé nán guā
这 里 有 冬 瓜 、 黄 瓜 、 西 瓜 , 和 南 瓜 。
Here are winter squash, cucumber, **watermelon**, and pumpkin.

774 吸   xī   **Verb:** to breathe; to suck

diàn yǐng lǐ de xī xuè guǐ zài xī xuè tài kě pà le
电 影 里 的 吸 血 鬼 在 吸 血 , 太 可 怕 了 !
The vampires in the movie are **sucking** blood, so scary!

775 吸管   xī guǎn   **Noun: straw**

hē zhēn zhū nǎi chá de shí hòu, wǒ xǐ huān yòng xī guǎn
喝 珍 珠 奶 茶 的 时 候， 我 喜 欢 用 **吸 管**。
When drinking bubble tea, I like to use a **straw**.

776 吸收   xī shōu   **Verb: to absorb; to take in**

tài yáng huā xū yào xī shōu yáng guāng cái néng kāi huā
太 阳 花 需 要 **吸 收** 阳 光 才 能 开 花。
Sunflowers need **to take in** sunlight to bloom.

777 吸烟   xī yān   **Verb: to smoke**

wǒ cóng lái bù xī yān, yīn wèi zhè duì jiàn kāng bù hǎo
我 从 来 不 **吸 烟**， 因 为 这 对 健 康 不 好。
I never **smoke** because it's bad for the health.

778 吸引   xī yǐn   **Verb: to attract**

wǒ dì yī cì jiàn dào tā de shí hòu, jiù bèi tā xī
我 第 一 次 见 到 他 的 时 候， 就 被 他 **吸**
yǐn le
引 了。
I was **attracted** to him the first time I saw him.

779 喜爱   xǐ ài   **Verb: be fond of**

nǐ zuì xǐ ài de qiǎo kè lì pái zi shì shén me
你 最 **喜 爱** 的 巧 克 力 牌 子 是 什 么 ？
What is your favorite (most **fond**) brand of chocolate?

780 系列   xì liè   **Noun:** series

^{wǒ} 我 ^{bà} 爸 ^{shì} 是 《^{dié}碟 ^{zhōng}中 ^{dié}谍》 ^{diàn}电 ^{yǐng}影 ^{xì}系 ^{liè}列 ^{de}的 ^{fěn}粉 ^{sī}丝。

My dad is a fan of the "Mission: Impossible" movie **series**.

---

781 系统   xì tǒng   **Noun:** system
                                   Adjective: systematic

Noun
什么？公司的网络系统奔溃了？
shén me ? gōng sī de wǎng luò xì tǒng bēn kuì le

What? The company's network **system** crashed?

Adj.
我们要对这个问题做系统的检查。
wǒ men yào duì zhè gè wèn tí zuò xì tǒng de jiǎn chá

We need to conduct a **systematic** examination of this issue.

---

782 细   xì   **Adjective:** thin; slender

这根针太粗，请换一根细的。
zhè gēn zhēn tài cū , qǐng huàn yì gēn xì de

This needle is too thick, please replace it with a **thin** one.

---

783 细节   xì jié   **Noun:** details

她是个注重细节的人，非常可靠。
tā shì gè zhù zhòng xì jié de rén , fēi cháng kě kào

She is a person who pays atention to **details** and very reliable.

---

784 细致   xì zhì   **Adjective:** delicate; meticulous

这件工艺品的做工很细致。
zhè jiàn gōng yì pǐn de zuò gōng hěn xì zhì

The workmanship of this handicraft is very **delicate**.

785 下个月   xià gè yuè   **Noun:** next month

lǎo bǎn shàng gè yuè zài bā lí xià gè yuè zài mǐ lán
老 板 上 个 月 在 巴 黎 ， **下 个 月** 在 米 兰 。
The boss was in Paris last month and Milan **next month**.

786 下降   xià jiàng   **Verb:** to decrease; to drop; to go down

fáng dài lì xī shàng zhǎng le wǒ xī wàng tā kuài diǎn xià jiàng
房 贷 利 息 上 涨 了 ， 我 希 望 它 快 点 **下 降** 。
Mortgage interest has gone up, I hope it **goes down** soon.

787 下楼   xià lóu   **Verb:** to go downstairs

nǐ kě yǐ cóng zhè lǐ xià lóu xǐ shǒu jiān zài dì xià shì
你 可 以 从 这 里 **下 楼** ， 洗 手 间 在 地 下 室 。
You can **go downstairs** from here, the toilet is in the basement.

788 下载   xià zǎi   **Verb:** to download

qǐng xiān xià zǎi fēng miàn rán hòu shàng chuán shì pín
请 先 **下 载** 封 面 ， 然 后 上 传 视 频 。
Please **download** the cover first, then upload the video.

789 夏季   xià jì   **Noun:** summer

měi nián xià jì wǒ men dōu huì cān jiā shā tān jù huì
每 年 **夏 季** ， 我 们 都 会 参 加 沙 滩 聚 会 。
Every **summer** we always attend the beach party.

790 鲜   xiān   **Adjective:** fresh; bright

wǒ zài mǔ qīn jié gěi mā ma zuò le yì pán xiān guǒ
我 在 母 亲 节 给 妈 妈 做 了 一 盘 **鲜** 果 。
I made a plate of **fresh** fruits for my mother on Mother's Day.

791 鲜花   xiān huā   **Noun:** flower (fresh)

zài qíng rén jié, wǒ de xiān shēng gěi wǒ mǎi le yí shù
在 情 人 节, 我 的 先 生 给 我 买 了 一 束
xiān huā
鲜 花 。

On Valentine's Day, my husband bought me a bouquet of **flowers.**

792 鲜明   xiān míng   **Adjective:** distinct

tā fēi cháng dú lì, gè xìng fēi cháng xiān míng
他 非 常 独 立, 个 性 非 常 鲜 明 。

He is very independent and has a very **distinct** personality.

793 咸   xián   **Adjective:** salty

zhè kuài niú pái yǒu diǎn xián, wèi dào tài zhòng le
这 块 牛 排 有 点 咸, 味 道 太 重 了 !

This steak was a little **salty** and the flavor is too heavy!

794 显著   xiǎn zhù   **Adjective:** remarkable (for things)

zhè chǎng zhàn zhēng shì lì shǐ shàng xiǎn zhù de dà shì
这 场 战 争 是 历 史 上 显 著 的 大 事 。

This war is a **remarkable** event in history.

795 县   xiàn   **Noun:** county

wǒ jì de tā hǎo xiàng lái zì xī běi de yí gè xiàn
我 记 得 他 好 像 来 自 西 北 的 一 个 县 。

I remember he seemed to be from a **county** in the northwest.

796 限制 xiàn zhì **Verb:** to limit

jì zhù, méi yǒu rén néng xiàn zhì nǐ de chuàng zào lì
记 住， 没 有 人 能 **限 制** 你 的 创 造 力 。
Remember, no one can **limit** your creativity.

797 相处 xiāng chǔ **Verb:** to get along with

wǒ gēn shì yǒu men xiāng chǔ de hěn hǎo, bié dān xīn
我 跟 室 友 们 **相 处** 得 很 好， 别 担 心 。
I **get on** very well **with** my roommates, don't worry.

798 相反 xiāng fǎn **Adjective:** contrary; opposite

tā xīn lǐ xiǎng de hé zuǐ lǐ shuō de shì xiāng fǎn de
她 心 里 想 的 和 嘴 里 说 的 是 **相 反** 的 。
What she thinks in her heart is the **opposite** of what she says from her mouth.

799 箱 xiāng **Classifier** for big containers

wǒ zài wǎng shàng mǎi le yì xiāng pí jiǔ, yí gòng yǒu píng
我 在 网 上 买 了 一 **箱** 啤 酒， 一 共 有12瓶 。
I bought a **box** of beer online, with 12 bottles in total.

800 箱子 xiāng zi **Noun:** box; case

bié rēng, zhè gè zhǐ xiāng zi kě yǐ huí shōu
别 扔， 这 个 纸 **箱 子** 可 以 回 收 。
Don't throw it away, this cardboard **box** can be recycled.

801 想(念) xiǎng niàn **Verb:** to miss (yearning)

wǒ xiǎng niàn jiā xiāng de měi jǐng hé měi shí
我 **想 念** 家 乡 的 美 景 和 美 食 。
I **miss** the beautiful scenery and delicious food of my hometown.

802 想象　　xiǎng xiàng

Verb: to imagine
Noun: imagination

Verb
wǒ wú fǎ xiǎng xiàng tā shì rú hé pò chǎn de
我 无 法 想 象 他 是 如 何 破 产 的 。
I can't **imagine** how he became broke.

Noun
zhè me dà de jīng jì sǔn shī chāo guò le tā de xiǎng xiàng
这 么 大 的 经 济 损 失 超 过 了 他 的 想 象 。
Such a large economic loss exceeded his **imagination**.

803 项　　xiàng

Classifier for tasks or agreements
Noun: neck (classical Chinese)

Class.
wǒ zài huì yì shàng gěi tóng shì men fēn pèi le jǐ xiàng
我 在 会 议 上 给 同 事 们 分 配 了 几 项
rèn wù
任 务 。
I assigned several tasks to colleagues in the meeting.

Noun
zhè tiáo jīn xiàng liàn shì tā sòng gěi wǒ de shēng rì lǐ wù
这 条 金 项 链 是 他 送 给 我 的 生 日 礼 物 。
This gold **neck**lace was his birthday present to me.

804 项目　　xiàng mù

Noun: project

wǒ tīng shuō wǒ men de xiàng mù jīng lǐ gāng gāng bèi chǎo le
我 听 说 我 们 的 项 目 经 理 刚 刚 被 炒 了 。
I heard that our **project** manager just got fired.

805 相片　　xiàng piàn

Noun: photo; photograph

tā fā huǒ le sī huǐ le zhè zhāng xiàng piàn
他 发 火 了 ， 撕 毁 了 这 张 相 片 。
He was mad and tore up the **photo**.

806 消化　　xiāo huà　　**Verb:** to digest　**Noun:** digestion

Verb
chī shén me kě yǐ bāng zhù xiāo huà zhī fáng
吃 什 么 可 以 帮 助 **消 化** 脂 肪 ？
What to eat to help **digest** fat?

Noun
zuì jìn wǒ de xiāo huà xì tǒng bú tài hǎo
最 近 我 的 **消 化** 系 统 不 太 好 。
Recently my **digestion** system is not so good.

807 销售　　xiāo shòu　　**Verb:** to sell　**Noun:** sales

Verb
nǐ kàn qián miàn de tān zi zài xiāo shòu xiāng bīn jiǔ
你 看 ， 前 面 的 摊 子 在 **销 售** 香 槟 酒 。
Look, the stall front is **selling** champagne.

Noun
zhè shì gōng sī de jì dù xiāo shòu bào gào
这 是 公 司 的 季 度 **销 售** 报 告 。
This is the company's quarterly **sales** report.

808 小吃　　xiāo chī　　**Noun:** snack

wǒ zuì xǐ huān de xiǎo chī shì yóu tiáo hé mán tou
我 最 喜 欢 的 **小 吃** 是 油 条 和 馒 头 。
My favorite **snacks** are fried dough sticks and steamed buns.

809 小伙子　　xiǎo huǒ zi　　**Noun:** young guy

zhè gè xiǎo huǒ zi mǎi le yí liàng lán bó jī ní pǎo chē
这 个 **小 伙 子** 买 了 一 辆 兰 博 基 尼 跑 车 。
The **young guy** bought a Lamborghini sports car.

810 小型　　xiǎo xíng　　**Adjective:** small-size; small-scale

nà liàng chē shì zhōng xíng de bú shì xiǎo xíng de
那 辆 车 是 中 型 的 ， 不 是 **小 型** 的 。
That car is a midsize one, not a **small-size** one.

811 效率 xiào lǜ **Noun:** efficiency

wǒ yào xiǎng bàn fǎ tí gāo wǒ de gōng zuò xiào lǜ
我 要 想 办 法 提 高 我 的 工 作 **效 率**。
I need to find ways to improve my work **efficiency**.

812 些 xiē **Classifier** for things or people: some; a few

yǒu xiē yuán gōng qù fēn gōng sī péi xùn le
有 **些** 员 工 去 分 公 司 培 训 了。
Some employees went to the company branch for training.

813 心理 xīn lǐ **Noun:** psychology

tā yù yuē le yí wèi xīn lǐ yī shēng
他 预 约 了 一 位 **心 理** 医 生。
He booked an appointment with a psychiatrist (**psychology** doctor).

814 新郎 xīn láng **Noun:** groom

zhè gè bàn láng shì xīn láng de dà xué tóng xué
这 个 伴 郎 是 **新 郎** 的 大 学 同 学。
This best man is the **groom**'s college classmate.

815 新娘 xīn niáng **Noun:** bride

shè yǐng shī zài gěi xīn niáng hé bàn niáng men pāi zhào
摄 影 师 在 给 **新 娘** 和 伴 娘 们 拍 照。
The photographer is taking pictures of the **bride** and bridesmaids.

816 新鲜 xīn xiān **Adjective:** fresh

bào yǔ tíng hòu kōng qì fēi cháng xīn xiān
暴 雨 停 后， 空 气 非 常 **新 鲜**。
After the heavy rain stopped, the air is very **fresh**.

817 新型　　xīn xíng　　**Adjective:** new type; new kind

zhè liàng chē shì gōng sī tuī chū de **xīn xíng** diàn dòng chē
这 辆 车 是 公 司 推 出 的 **新 型** 电 动 车 。
This car is a **new** electric car launched by the company.

818 兴奋　　xīng fèn　　**Adjective:** excited　**Noun:** excitement

Adj.
wǒ xiāng xìn gù kè men kàn dào tā huì fēi cháng **xīng fèn**
我 相 信 顾 客 们 看 到 它 会 非 常 **兴 奋** 。
I'm sure customers will be very **excited** to see it.

Noun
xiàn zài tā de nèi xīn chōng mǎn **xīng fèn** hé jī qíng
现 在 他 的 内 心 充 满 **兴 奋** 和 激 情 。
Now his inner heart is full of **excitement** and passion.

819 形容　　xíng róng　　**Verb:** to describe　**Noun:** description

Verb
qǐng **xíng róng** nǐ zuì xǐ huān de shè jì fēng gé
请 **形 容** 你 最 喜 欢 的 设 计 风 格 。
Please **describe** your favorite design style.

Noun
nǐ de **xíng róng** fēi cháng shēng dòng wǒ zhōng yú míng bái le
你 的 **形 容** 非 常 生 动 ！ 我 终 于 明 白 了 ！
Your **description** is very vivid! I finally understand!

820 形势　　xíng shì　　**Noun:** situation (formal)

zhè lǐ de zhèng zhì hé jīng jì **xíng shì** dōu bù hǎo
这 里 的 政 治 和 经 济 **形 势** 都 不 好 。
The political and economic **situation** here are both not good.

821 型　　xíng　　**Noun:** model; type

duì le nǐ de xuè **xíng** shì shén me
对 了 ， 你 的 血 **型** 是 什 么 ？
By the way, what is your blood **type**?

822 型号   xíng hào   **Noun:** model (of product)

qǐng gào sù wǒ nǐ chē zi de xíng hào hé chē pái hào
请 告 诉 我 你 车 子 的 **型 号** 和 车 牌 号。
Please tell me the **model** and license plate number of your car.

823 醒   xǐng   **Verb:** to wake up

yīn wèi shí chā wǒ líng chén sān diǎn jiù xǐng le
因 为 时 差， 我 凌 晨 三 点 就 **醒** 了。
Because of jet lag, I **woke up** at 3am.

824 兴趣   xìng qù   **Noun:** interest

zhè gè huā huā gōng zǐ zhǐ duì měi nǚ yǒu xìng qù
这 个 花 花 公 子 只 对 美 女 有 **兴 趣**。
This playboy only has **interest** in beautiful women.

825 性质   xìng zhì   **Noun:** nature (of things)

nǐ yīng gāi kàn qīng zhè gè wèn tí de xìng zhì
你 应 该 看 清 这 个 问 题 的 **性 质**。
You should see the **nature** of this problem clearly.

826 兄弟   xiōng dì   **Noun:** brother; close mates

tā bù jǐn shì wǒ de péng yǒu yě shì wǒ de xiōng dì
他 不 仅 是 我 的 朋 友， 也 是 我 的 **兄 弟**。
He's not only my friend but also a **brother** to me.

827 胸部   xiōng bù   **Noun:** chest; breast

tā de xiōng bù hěn dà yīn wèi yǒu hěn duō jī ròu
他 的 **胸 部** 很 大， 因 为 有 很 多 肌 肉。
His **chest** is big because there are a lot of muscles.

828 修理 xiū lǐ — **Verb:** to fix; to repair

zāo gāo wǒ men de kā fēi jī huài le xū yào xiū lǐ
糟 糕 ！ 我 们 的 咖 啡 机 坏 了 ， 需 要 **修 理** 。
Oops! Our coffee machine is broken and needs **repairing**.

829 选择 xuǎn zé — **Verb:** to choose / **Noun:** choice

Verb
wǒ jiě hé jiě fū xuǎn zé bú yào hái zi
我 姐 和 姐 夫 **选 择** 不 要 孩 子 。
My older sister and brother-in-law **chose** not to have kids.

Noun
děng tā men lǎo le kě néng huì hòu huǐ zhè gè xuǎn zé
等 他 们 老 了 ， 可 能 会 后 悔 这 个 **选 择** 。
When they are old, they may regret this **choice**.

830 学分 xué fēn — **Noun:** academic credit

tā hěn yōu xiù xué fēn shì bān lǐ zuì gāo de
他 很 优 秀 ， **学 分** 是 班 里 最 高 的 ！
He is excellent, and his **credits** are the highest in the class!

831 学年 xué nián — **Noun:** school year; academic year

zài zhè gè xué nián wǒ shè lì le sān gè mù biāo
在 这 个 **学 年** ， 我 设 立 了 三 个 目 标 。
For this **school year**, I've set three goals.

832 学时 xué shí — **Noun:** class hour

zài dà xué tā měi tiān shàng bā gè xué shí de zhōng wén kè
在 大 学 他 每 天 上 八 个 **学 时** 的 中 文 课 。
Every day at the university he has 8 **class hours** of Chinese classes.

833 学术　　　xué shù　　　**Noun: academic**

jiào xué lóu zhèng zài jǔ xíng xué shù tǎo lùn
教 学 楼 正 在 举 行 **学 术** 讨 论 。
Academic discussions are being held in the teaching building.

834 学问　　　xué wèn　　　**Noun: knowledge (academic)**

tā shì běi jīng dà xué de jiào shòu yǒu hěn shēn de xué wèn
他 是 北 京 大 学 的 教 授 ， 有 很 深 的 **学 问** 。
He is a professor at Peking University and has profound **knowledge**.

835 寻找　　　xún zhǎo　　　**Verb: to seek; to look for; to find**

tā zài sì shí suì de shí hòu xún zhǎo dào le zhēn ài
他 在 四 十 岁 的 时 候 **寻 找** 到 了 真 爱 。
He **found** his true love when he was forty years old.

836 迅速　　　xùn sù　　　**Adjective: rapid; fast**

zài gāo sù gōng lù shàng wǒ kāi chē kāi de hěn xùn sù
在 高 速 公 路 上 ， 我 开 车 开 得 很 **迅 速** 。
On the highway, I drive my car very **fast**.

837 牙　　　yá　　　**Noun: tooth**

shén me tā chī fàn de shí hòu yá diào le
什 么 ？ 他 吃 饭 的 时 候 ， **牙** 掉 了 ？
What? When he was eating, his **tooth** fell out?

838 牙刷　　　yá shuā　　　**Noun: toothbrush**

zhè gè diàn dòng yá shuā yǒu diǎn guì yào měi yuán
这 个 电 动 **牙 刷** 有 点 贵 ， 要 295 美 元 。
This electric **toothbrush** is a bit expensive, it costs $295.

839 亚运会   yà yùn huì   **Noun:** Asian Games

wǒ men hěn qī dài kàn yà yùn huì de kāi mù shì
我 们 很 期 待 看 **亚 运 会** 的 开 幕 式 。
We looking forward seeing the opening ceremony of the **Asian Games**.

840 呀   ya   **Interjection:** ah

ya zhōng guó zhǔ xí yě huì chū xí
呀！中 国 主 席 也 会 出 席 。
Ah! The President of China will also be present.

841 延长   yán cháng   **Verb:** to extend

zǒng jīng lǐ xī wàng yán cháng hé tong qī xiàn
总 经 理 希 望 **延 长** 合 同 期 限 。
The CEO wants to **extend** the contract period.

842 延期   yán qī   **Verb:** to delay; to postpone

wèi le bì kāi bào fēng xuě pǎo chē bǐ sài bèi yán qī le
为 了 避 开 暴 风 雪 ， 跑 车 比 赛 被 **延 期** 了 。
To avoid the blizzard, the sports car race is **postponed**.

843 延续   yán xù   **Verb:** to continue; to last (formal)

zhōng huá wén míng yán xù le wǔ qiān nián
中 华 文 明 **延 续** 了 五 千 年 。
Chinese civilization has **lasted** for five thousand years.

844 严   yán   **Adjective:** harsh; tight; stern

wǒ de péng yǒu zuǐ yán bú huì xiè lù zhè gè mì mì
我 的 朋 友 嘴 **严** ， 不 会 泄 露 这 个 秘 密 。
My friend is **tight**-lipped and will not leak this secret.

845 严格 yán gé **Adjective:** strict

wǒ jué de bān zhǔ rèn duì xué shēng men bú gòu yán gé
我 觉 得 班 主 任 对 学 生 们 不 够 **严 格** 。
I think the head teacher is not **strict** enough with the students.

846 严重 yán zhòng **Adjective:** serious (bad)

xiào zhǎng chū chē huò le bìng qíng yǒu diǎn yán zhòng
校 长 出 车 祸 了 ， 病 情 有 点 **严 重** 。
The principle got into a car accident, his condition is a bit **serious**.

847 研究 yán jiū **Verb:** to research
Noun: research

Verb
kē xué jiā men zài yán jiū zhè gè bìng dú de yì miáo
科 学 家 们 在 **研 究** 这 个 病 毒 的 疫 苗 。
Scientists are **researching** a vaccine for this virus.

Noun
wǒ xī wàng tā men de yán jiū kuài diǎn chū jié guǒ
我 希 望 他 们 的 **研 究** 快 点 出 结 果 。
I hope their **research** yields results soon.

848 研究生 yán jiū shēng **Noun:** postgraduate; graduate student

zhè lǐ yǒu běn kē shēng yán jiū shēng hé bó shì shēng
这 里 有 本 科 生 、 **研 究 生** 和 博 士 生 。
There are undergraduates, **postgraduates** and doctoral students here.

849 研制 yán zhì **Verb:** to develop (from research)

zhè shì ōu lái yǎ gōng sī yán zhì de hù fū pǐn
这 是 欧 莱 雅 公 司 **研 制** 的 护 肤 品 。
This is a skin care product **developed** by L'Oréal.

850 盐   yán   **Noun:** salt

wǒ yào jiā yán   hú jiāo fěn hé fān jiā jiàng
我 要 加 **盐**、胡 椒 粉 和 番 茄 酱。
I'll add **salt**, pepper and tomato ketchup.

851 眼镜   yǎn jìng   **Noun:** glasses

wǒ kāi chē de shí hòu yào dài yǎn jìng
我 开 车 的 时 候 要 戴 **眼 镜**。
I need to wear **glasses** when I drive.

852 眼泪   yǎn lèi   **Noun:** tear; teardrop

tā hé nán péng yǒu fēn shǒu le   suǒ yǐ liú yǎn lèi
她 和 男 朋 友 分 手 了，所 以 流 **眼 泪**。
She broke up with her boyfriend, so she shed **tears**.

853 眼里   yǎn lǐ   in one's eyes

zài wǒ yǎn lǐ   tā men yì zhí hěn xiāng ài
在 我 **眼 里**，他 们 一 直 很 相 爱。
In my eyes, they have always been very in love.

854 演讲   yǎn jiǎng   **Verb:** to give a speech   **Noun:** speech

Verb
měi cì yǎn jiǎng   wǒ dōu fēi cháng jǐn zhāng
每 次 **演 讲**，我 都 非 常 紧 张。
Every time I **give a speech**, I feel very nervous.

Noun
zhōu zhǎng de yǎn jiǎng zài guó huì shàng hěn shòu huān yíng
州 长 的 **演 讲** 在 国 会 上 很 受 欢 迎。
The governor's **speech** was very popular in Congress.

855 阳台   yáng tái   **Noun:** balcony

wǒ de gōng yù yǒu yí gè yáng tái shài yī fu hěn fāng biàn
我 的 公 寓 有 一 个 **阳 台**，晒 衣 服 很 方 便。
My apartment has a **balcony**; drying clothes is convenient.

856 养成   yǎng chéng   **Verb:** to cultivate or form (personality or habits)

wǒ xī wàng hái zi néng yǎng chéng zǎo shuì zǎo qǐ de xí guàn
我 希 望 孩 子 能 **养 成** 早 睡 早 起 的 习 惯。
I want my kids **to form** the habit of sleeping and getting up early.

857 腰   yāo   **Noun:** waist

qǐng wèn nǐ de xiōng wéi hé yāo wéi shì duō shǎo
请 问， 你 的 胸 围 和 **腰** 围 是 多 少 ？
May I ask, what is your bust size and **waist** size?

858 摇   yáo   **Verb:** to shake

wǒ zài xiě zì tīng huà bié yáo wǒ de zhuō zi
我 在 写 字， 听 话， 别 **摇** 我 的 桌 子。
I am writing, behave, don't **shake** my table.

859 药物   yào wù   **Noun:** medicine

wǒ jué de zhè xiē yào wù de xiào guǒ bú tài hǎo
我 觉 得 这 些 **药 物** 的 效 果 不 太 好。
I think these **medicines** don't have much effect.

860 要是   yào shì   **Conjunction:** if

yào shì chī tā men wú xiào jiù qù kàn yī shēng ba
要 是 吃 它 们 无 效， 就 去 看 医 生 吧。
If eating them is not effective, just go to see a doctor.

861 业余　yè yú　**Adjective:** amateur; spare time

zài yè yú shí jiān wǒ xǐ huān dǎ wǎng qiú nǐ ne
在业余时间，我喜欢打网球，你呢？
In my **spare time**, I like to play tennis, how about you?

862 叶子　yè zi　**Noun:** leaf

tā sòng le wǒ yí duì yín yè zi ěr huán
他送了我一对银叶子耳环。
He gifted me a pair of silver **leaf** earrings.

863 医疗　yī liáo　**Noun:** medical; medical treatment

zhè jiā yī yuàn de yī liáo shè bèi hěn xiān jìn
这家医院的医疗设备很先进。
The **medical** equipment in this hospital is very advanced.

864 医学　yī xué　**Noun:** medical science

tā men yǒu hěn duō bù tóng lǐng yù de yī xué zhuān jiā
他们有很多不同领域的医学专家。
They have many **medical** experts in different fields.

865 依靠　yī kào　**Verb:** to rely on; to depend on

wǒ de nán péng yǒu hěn dú lì bù yī kào tā de fù mǔ
我的男朋友很独立，不依靠他的父母。
My boyfriend is independent and doesn't **depend on** his parents.

866 依然　yī rán　**Adverb:** still

tā shí bā suì de shí hòu yī rán yí gè rén zhù
他十八岁的时候，依然一个人住。
When he was eighteen, he **still** lived alone.

867 一律 yí lǜ — Adverb: all (and singular)

qián miàn fēng lù le, chē zi yí lǜ bù zhǔn jìn rù
前 面 封 路 了, 车 子 一 律 不 准 进 入 。
The road ahead is closed; **all** cars are not allowed to enter.

868 一再 yí zài — Adverb: repeatedly

tā yí zài wéi guī, yǐ jīng bèi fá kuǎn le
他 一 再 违 规 , 已 经 被 罚 款 了 。
He has **repeatedly** violated the rules and has been fined.

869 一致 yí zhì — Adjective: identical; consistent / Adverb: together; all

Adj.
wǒ men de xìn yǎng hé jià zhí guān yí zhì
我 们 的 信 仰 和 价 值 观 一 致 。
Our beliefs and values are **consistent**.

Adv.
wǒ men yí zhì tóng yì míng nián xià tiān bān jiā
我 们 一 致 同 意 明 年 夏 天 搬 家 。
We have **all** agreed to move house next summer.

870 移 yí — Verb: to move

bǎ shǔ biāo yí guò lái, wǒ jiāo nǐ zěn me xià zǎi
把 鼠 标 移 过 来 , 我 教 你 怎 么 下 载 。
Move the mouse over and I will teach you how to download.

871 移动 yí dòng — Verb: to shift

lóng juǎn fēng yí dòng de hěn kuài, kě néng huì yǐng xiǎng zhè lǐ
龙 卷 风 移 动 得 很 快 , 可 能 会 影 响 这 里 。
Tornadoes **shift** very quickly and could affect this area.

872 移民　yí mín
Verb: to immigrate
Noun: immigrant; immigration

Verb
tā men zài jiǔ shí nián dài jiù yí mín měi guó le
他 们 在 九 十 年 代 就 移 民 美 国 了 。
They **immigrated** to the United States in the 1990s.

Noun
yí mín shǒu xù hěn fù zá　wǒ yào qǐng lǜ shī bāng máng
移 民 手 续 很 复 杂 ， 我 要 请 律 师 帮 忙 。
The **immigration** procedures are complex, I need to ask a lawyer for help.

873 遗产　yí chǎn
Noun: heritage; inheritance

tīng shuō tā jì chéng le yì bǎi wàn měi yuán de yí chǎn
听 说 他 继 承 了 一 百 万 美 元 的 遗 产 。
I heard that he inherited a million dollars' **inheritance**.

874 遗传　yí chuán
Verb: to pass down (trait or disease through inheritance)

tā de táng niào bìng shì tā mā yí chuán gěi tā de
他 的 糖 尿 病 是 他 妈 遗 传 给 他 的 。
His diabetes was **passed down** to him by his mother.

875 疑问　yí wèn
Noun: doubt; question

rú guǒ nín yǒu yí wèn　qǐng suí shí lián xì wǒ
如 果 您 有 疑 问 ， 请 随 时 联 系 我 。
If you have **questions**, please contact me anytime.

876 以及　yǐ jí
Conjunction: as well as; and (formal)

wǒ de tuán duì yǐ jí wǒ dōu huì tí gōng bāng zhù
我 的 团 队 以 及 我 都 会 提 供 帮 助 。
My team **and** I will provide assistance.

877 以内　　yǐ nèi　　within

wǒ men dǎ suàn zài liǎng nián yǐ nèi ān dìng xià lái
我 们 打 算 在 两 年 **以 内** 安 定 下 来 。
We intend to settle down **within** two years.

878 一般来说　　yì bān lái shuō　　**Phrase:** generally speaking

yì bān lái shuō nǚ rén bǐ nán rén gèng xiǎng jié hūn
一 般 来 说 ， 女 人 比 男 人 更 想 结 婚 。
Generally speaking, women want to get married more than men.

879 义务　　yì wù　　**Noun:** obligation; responsibility

yǒu hái zi hòu fù mǔ yào chéng dān de yì wù gèng duō
有 孩 子 后 ， 父 母 要 承 担 的 **义 务** 更 多 。
After having children, parents have more **responsibilities** to bear.

880 议论　　yì lùn　　**Verb:** to discuss (formal) **Noun:** discussion

Verb

tā men zài yì lùn dāng dài hūn yīn hé jiā tíng wèn tí
他 们 在 **议 论** 当 代 婚 姻 和 家 庭 问 题 。
They were **discussing** contemporary marriage and family issues.

Noun

wǒ jué de zhè cì de yì lùn fēi cháng yǒu yì yì
我 觉 得 这 次 的 **议 论** 非 常 有 意 义 。
I think this time's **discussion** is very meaningful.

881 引　　yǐn　　**Verb:** to lead

yǒu dǎo yóu yóu wèi wǒ men yǐn lù bú yòng dān xīn mí lù
有 导 游 为 我 们 **引** 路 ， 不 用 担 心 迷 路 。
There is a tour guide **leading** us, no need to worry about getting lost.

882 引导   yǐn dǎo   **Verb:** to guide
Noun: guidance

Verb
tuán duì lǐng dǎo zài yǐn dǎo dà jiā wán chéng rèn wù
团 队 领 导 在 引 导 大 家 完 成 任 务 。
The team leader is **guiding** everyone to complete the task.

Noun
wǒ men hěn gǎn jī yǒu tā de yǐn dǎo
我 们 很 感 激 有 他 的 引 导 。
We are grateful to have his **guidance**.

883 引进   yǐn jìn   **Verb:** to introduce; to bring in

gōng sī zuì jìn yǐn jìn le zuì xīn de gāo kē jì
公 司 最 近 引 进 了 最 新 的 高 科 技 。
The company has recently **introduced** the latest high-tech.

884 引起   yǐn qǐ   **Verb:** to cause

tóu zī shī bài yǐn qǐ le gōng sī de cái wù wēi jī
投 资 失 败 引 起 了 公 司 的 财 务 危 机 。
The failure of the investment **caused** the company's financial crisis.

885 应(该)   yīng gāi   **Phrase:** should; ought to

zuò jué dìng zhī qián nǐ yìng quán héng lì bì
做 决 定 之 前 , 你 应 权 衡 利 弊 。
Before making a decision, you **should** weigh the pros and cons.

886 英勇   yīng yǒng   **Adjective:** heroic

tā shì bǎo hù dà jiā de zhēn yīng xióng fēi cháng yīng yǒng
他 是 保 护 大 家 的 真 英 雄 , 非 常 英 勇 。
He is a true hero who protects everyone, very **heroic**.

887 营业   yíng yè   **Verb:** to operate (business running)

shāng diàn zhōu yī dào zhōu liù yíng yè   zhōu rì guān mén
商 店 周 一 到 周 六 营 业， 周 日 关 门 。
The store **operates** Monday to Saturday and closes on Sunday.

---

888 赢得   yíng dé   **Verb:** to gain; to win

jīng guò liǎng nián de zhuī qiú， tā zhōng yú yíng dé le tā
经 过 两 年 的 追 求， 他 终 于 赢 得 了 她
de xīn
的 心 。
After two years of courtship, he finally **won** her heart.

---

889 影子   yǐng zi   **Noun:** shadow

bù guǎn wǒ qù nǎ， wǒ de gǒu jiù xiàng yǐng zi yí yàng
不 管 我 去 哪， 我 的 狗 就 像 影 子 一 样
gēn zhe wǒ
跟 着 我 。
Wherever I go, my dog follows me like a **shadow**.

---

890 勇敢   yǒng gǎn   **Adjective:** brave

tā shì wǒ jiàn guò de zuì yǒng gǎn de rén
他 是 我 见 过 的 最 勇 敢 的 人 。
He is the bravest (most **brave**) man I have ever met.

---

891 勇气   yǒng qì   **Noun:** courage; bravery

wǒ hěn xīn shǎng tā de yǒng qì hé zhì huì
我 很 欣 赏 他 的 勇 气 和 智 慧 。
I really appreciate his **courage** and wisdom.

892 用途　　yòng tú　　**Noun:** utility; use; purpose

chú le zhuāng shì　zhè gè xiǎo huā píng méi shén me yòng tú
除了装饰，这个小花瓶没什么**用途**。
Apart from decoration, this little vase has no other **use**.

893 优良　　yōu liáng　　**Adjective:** good (score or quality)

tā zhè cì de kǎo shì chéng jī yōu liáng　wǒ men hěn kāi xīn
他这次的考试成绩**优良**，我们很开心。
We are very happy that his exam score is **good** this time.

894 优美　　yōu měi　　**Adjective:** graceful; beautiful (for things)

zhè shǒu zhōng wén gē hěn yōu měi　nǐ yě tīng tīng ba
这首中文歌很**优美**，你也听听吧。
This Chinese song is very **beautiful**; give it a listen too.

895 优秀　　yōu xiù　　**Adjective:** excellent

wǒ lǎo gōng shì yí gè yōu xiù de kuài jì shī
我老公是一个**优秀**的会计师。
My husband is an **excellent** accountant.

896 邮局　　yóu jú　　**Noun:** post office

wǒ jiā fù jìn yǒu yóu jú　méi yǒu jǐng chá jú
我家附近有**邮局**，没有警察局。
There is a **post office** near my house, but no police station.

897 有劲　　yǒu jìn　　**Adjective:** energetic (have strength)

wǒ xiàn zài méi jìn　chī fàn yǐ hòu cái yǒu jìn
我现在没劲，吃饭以后才**有劲**。
I have no strength now, I'll only be **energetic** after eating.

898 有趣 yǒu qù **Adjective:** interesting

wǒ jué de wán huá bǎn hěn méi qù kě shì tā jué de
我 觉 得 玩 滑 板 很 没 趣 ， 可 是 他 觉 得
yǒu qù
有 趣 。
I think skateboarding is boring, but he thinks it's **interesting**.

899 有限 yǒu xiàn **Adjective:** limited; finite

wǒ men de shí jiān shì yǒu xiàn de bú shì wú xiàn de
我 们 的 时 间 是 有 限 的 ， 不 是 无 限 的 。
Our time is **finite**, not infinite.

900 幼儿园 yòu ér yuán **Noun:** kindergarten

bǎo mǔ qù yòu ér yuán jiē wǒ nǚ ér le
保 姆 去 幼 儿 园 接 我 女 儿 了 。
The nanny went to the **kindergarten** to pick up my daughter.

901 于是 yú shì **Conjunction:** so; therefore

tā bú ài tā le yú shì tí chū le fēn shǒu
她 不 爱 他 了 ， 于 是 提 出 了 分 手 。
She didn't love him anymore, **so** she proposed to break up.

902 语法 yǔ fǎ **Noun:** grammar

qí shí zhōng wén de yǔ fǎ bú tài fù zá
其 实 ， 中 文 的 语 法 不 太 复 杂 。
In fact, Chinese **grammar** is not too complex.

903 语音   yǔ yīn   **Noun:** audio

qǐng wèn, zài nǎ lǐ kě yǐ xià zǎi yǔ yīn wén jiàn
请 问， 在 哪 里 可 以 下 载 **语音** 文 件 ？
Excuse me, where can I download the **audio** files?

904 玉   yù   **Noun:** jade

wǒ mǎi le yì zhī yù zhuó hé yì tiáo yù shí xiàng liàn
我 买 了 一 只 **玉** 镯 和 一 条 **玉** 石 项 链 。
I bought a **jade** bracelet and a **jade** necklace.

905 玉米   yù mǐ   **Noun:** corn

wǒ xǐ huān chī yù mǐ hé xī lán huā nǐ ne
我 喜 欢 吃 **玉 米** 和 西 兰 花， 你 呢 ？
I like to eat **corn** and broccoli, how about you?

906 预测   yù cè   **Verb:** to forecast; to predict
Noun: prognosis; prediction

Verb
zhuān jiā men yù cè kě néng huì fā shēng jīn róng wēi jī
专 家 们 **预 测** 可 能 会 发 生 金 融 危 机 。
Experts **predict** a financial crisis is likely to happen.

Noun
tā men de yù cè zhēn de zhǔn què ma
他 们 的 **预 测** 真 的 准 确 吗 ？
Are their **predictions** really accurate?

907 预订   yù dìng   **Verb:** to book

wǒ yǐ jīng yù dìng le míng nián qù zhōng guó de fēi jī piào
我 已 经 **预 订** 了 明 年 去 中 国 的 飞 机 票 。
I have already **booked** a flight ticket to China next year.

908 遇　　　　yù　　　**Verb:** to meet
(use with other words)

_{wǒ zuó tiān zài shì zhōng xīn ǒu yù le qián nán yǒu}
我 昨 天 在 市 中 心 偶 遇 了 前 男 友 。
I **met** my ex-boyfriend **by chance** yesterday downtown.

909 遇到　　　　yù dào　　　**Verb:** to encounter

_{yù dào tā ràng wǒ gǎn jué yǒu diǎn gān gà}
遇 到 他 让 我 感 觉 有 点 尴 尬 ！
Encountering him made me feel a little embarrassed!

910 遇见　　　　yù jiàn　　　**Verb:** to come across

_{wǒ zài fēi jī shàng yù jiàn le yí wèi hǎo lái wù míng xīng}
我 在 飞 机 上 遇 见 了 一 位 好 莱 坞 明 星 。
I **came across** a Hollywood star on the plane.

911 原料　　　　yuán liào　　　**Noun:** raw material

_{zhè xiē gāng tiě yuán liào shì cóng zhōng guó jìn kǒu de}
这 些 钢 铁 原 料 是 从 中 国 进 口 的 。
These steel **raw materials** are imported from China.

912 原则　　　　yuán zé　　　**Noun:** principle

_{zài jiāo péng yǒu fāng miàn tā yǒu zì jǐ de yuán zé}
在 交 朋 友 方 面 ， 他 有 自 己 的 原 则 。
When it comes to making friends, he has his own **principles**.

913 圆　　　　yuán　　　**Adjective:** round;
circular

_{wǒ de chú fáng yǒu yì zhāng yuán zhuō zi hé sì bǎ yǐ zi}
我 的 厨 房 有 一 张 圆 桌 子 和 四 把 椅 子 。
My kitchen has a **round** table and four chairs.

914 圆满   yuán mǎn   **Adjective:** fulfilling; satisfactory

xìng kuī zhè bù diàn shì jù de jié jú hěn yuán mǎn
幸 亏 这 部 电 视 剧 的 结 局 很 **圆 满**!
Luckily this TV show had a **satisfactory** ending!

915 约会   yuē huì   **Verb:** to date
Noun: date; appointment

Verb
tā gēn zhè gè nǚ shēng yǐ jīng yuē huì bā gè yuè le
他 跟 这 个 女 生 已 经 **约 会** 八 个 月 了 。
He has been **dating** this girl for eight months.

Noun
wǒ gēn yī shēng de yuē huì gāng gāng bèi qǔ xiāo le
我 跟 医 生 的 **约 会** 刚 刚 被 取 消 了 。
My **appointment** with the doctor just got canceled.

916 月底   yuè dǐ   **Noun:** the end of a month

wǒ yuè dǐ yào qù dōng jīng cān jiā yí gè hūn lǐ
我 **月 底** 要 去 东 京 参 加 一 个 婚 礼 。
I will go to Tokyo to attend a wedding at the **end of the month**.

917 阅读   yuè dú   **Verb:** to read (formal)

wǒ yào shì zhe tí gāo wǒ de yuè dú sù dù
我 要 试 着 提 高 我 的 **阅 读** 速 度 。
I want to try to improve my **reading** speed.

918 运动会   yùn dòng huì   **Noun:** match; athletic meetings; sports game

zhè cì de ào lín pǐ kè yùn dòng huì zài nǎ lǐ jǔ xíng
这 次 的 奥 林 匹 克 **运 动 会** 在 哪 里 举 行 ?
Where is the Olympic **Games** held this time?

919 运动员 yùn dòng yuán **Noun:** athlete; sportsman

wǒ men tuán duì de yùn dòng yuán tiān tiān dōu zài xùn liàn
我 们 团 队 的 **运 动 员** 天 天 都 在 训 练 。
Athletes on our team are training every day.

920 运气 yùn qi **Noun:** luck

yíng dé guàn jūn bú shì kào yùn qi ér shì kào shí lì
赢 得 冠 军 不 是 靠 **运 气** ， 而 是 靠 实 力 。
Winning the championship doesn't rely on **luck**, but on strength.

921 运用 yùn yòng **Verb:** to apply
Noun: application

Verb
wǒ yì zhí yùn yòng zhè gè yuán zé jiě jué wèn tí
我 一 直 **运 用** 这 个 原 则 解 决 问 题 。
I always **apply** this principle to solve problems.

Noun
dàn shì wǒ hái méi yǒu wán quán zhǎng wò yùn yòng fāng fǎ
但 是 我 还 没 有 完 全 掌 握 **运 用** 方 法 。
But I haven't fully mastered the **application** method.

922 再三 zài sān **Adverb:** repeatedly; again and again

tā zài sān qiáng diào wǒ men yí dìng bù néng fàng qì
他 **再 三** 强 调 ： 我 们 一 定 不 能 放 弃 。
He emphasized **repeatedly**: We must not give up.

923 在乎 zài hu **Verb:** to care about

wǒ guān xīn nǐ de jiàn kāng yě zài hu nǐ de gǎn shòu
我 关 心 你 的 健 康 ， 也 **在 乎** 你 的 感 受 。
I care for your health and I **care about** your feelings.

924 在于   zài yú   **Verb:** lies in; to depend on

chéng gōng de guān jiàn zài yú zhèng què de fāng fǎ hé nǔ lì

成 功 的 关 键 **在 于** 正 确 的 方 法 和 努 力。

The key to success **lies in** the right approach and hard work.

925 赞成   zàn chéng   **Verb:** to approve; to agree

bǎi fēn zhī bā shí de rén zàn chéng zhè gè tí yì

百 分 之 八 十 的 人 **赞 成** 这 个 提 议。

Eighty percent of people **approve** this proposal.

926 赞赏   zàn shǎng   **Verb:** to praise
Noun: praise; admiration

Verb

lǎo shī men fēi cháng zàn shǎng tā de shū fǎ hé huì huà

老 师 们 非 常 **赞 赏** 他 的 书 法 和 绘 画。

The teachers heavily **praised** his calligraphy and paintings.

Noun

tā men de zàn shǎng ràng tā fēi cháng kāi xīn

他 们 的 **赞 赏** 让 他 非 常 开 心。

Their **admiration** made him very happy.

927 赞助   zàn zhù   **Verb:** to sponsor

wǒ men yǒu wǔ gè zàn zhù shāng zàn zhù zhè cì huó dòng

我 们 有 五 个 赞 助 商 **赞 助** 这 次 活 动。

We have five sponsors **sponsoring** the event.

928 造型   zào xíng   **Noun:** style; model; pose

hěn duō míng xīng zài pāi zhào de shí hòu dōu huì bǎi zào xíng

很 多 明 星 在 拍 照 的 时 候 都 会 摆 **造 型**。

Many celebrities will do **poses** when taking photos.

929 战斗　　zhàn dòu　　**Noun:** fight; battle; combat

jǐ qiān míng shì bīng zài zhàn dòu zhōng xī shēng le
几 千 名 士 兵 在 **战 斗** 中 牺 牲 了 。
Thousands of soldiers died in the **combat**.

930 战胜　　zhàn shèng　　**Verb:** to conquer; to defeat

tā men suī rán zhàn shèng le dí rén dàn shì sǔn shī hěn dà
他 们 虽 然 **战 胜** 了 敌 人 ， 但 是 损 失 很 大 。
Although they **defeated** the enemy, they suffered heavy losses.

931 战士　　zhàn shì　　**Noun:** warrior; soldier; fighter

zǒng tǒng wèi sǐ qù de zhàn shì jiàn lì le jì niàn bēi
总 统 为 死 去 的 **战 士** 建 立 了 纪 念 碑 。
The president has established a memorial for fallen **soldiers**.

932 战争　　zhàn zhēng　　**Noun:** war

wǒ men xī wàng shì jiè hé píng bú zài yǒu zhàn zhēng
我 们 希 望 世 界 和 平 ， 不 再 有 **战 争** 。
We want peace for the world and no more **wars**.

933 丈夫　　zhàng fu　　**Noun:** husband

tā men jié hūn le xiàn zài shì zhàng fu hé qī zi
他 们 结 婚 了 ， 现 在 是 **丈 夫** 和 妻 子 。
They got married and are now **husband** and wife.

934 招呼　　zhāo hu　　**Verb:** to greet; to notify

xīn láng hé xīn niáng zài dà tīng zhāo hu kè rén
新 郎 和 新 娘 在 大 厅 **招 呼** 客 人 。
The bride and groom are **greeting** guests in the hall.

935 着   zhe   **Particle:** indicate continuous action (verb + 着)

bàn láng hé bàn niáng dōu ná zhe jiǔ bēi
伴 郎 和 伴 娘 都 拿 着 酒 杯 。
The best man and bridesmaid were **holding** wine glasses.

936 着火   zháo huǒ   **Verb:** on fire

nà zuò gōng yù lóu zháo huǒ le kuài bào jǐng
那 座 公 寓 楼 着 火 了 ， 快 报 警 。
That apartment building is **on fire**, quickly call emergency services.

937 着急   zháo jí   **Adjective:** worry; anxious

bié zháo jí xiāo fáng duì huì mǎ shàng lái jiù huǒ
别 着 急 ， 消 防 队 会 马 上 来 救 火 。
Don't **worry**, the fire department will come to put out the fire right away.

938 召开   zhào kāi   **Verb:** to convene

rén mín dài biǎo dà huì yì zhí zài běi jīng zhào kāi
人 民 代 表 大 会 一 直 在 北 京 召 开 。
People's Congress has always **convened** in Beijing.

939 折   zhé   **Verb:** to fracture; to break; to fold

hěn yí hàn tā de tuǐ zài chē huò zhōng zhé le
很 遗 憾 ， 他 的 腿 在 车 祸 中 折 了 。
Unfortunately, his leg was **broken** in a car accident.

940 针   zhēn   **Noun:** needle; shot (injection)

wǒ wài pó hé wài gōng dōu dǎ le sān zhēn yì miáo
我 外 婆 和 外 公 都 打 了 三 针 疫 苗 。
My grandma and grandpa both had three **shots** of the vaccine.

941 针对   zhēn duì   **Verb:** to target; to aim at

gōng sī de chǎn pǐn zhǔ yào zhēn duì ōu měi shì chǎng
公 司 的 产 品 主 要 针 对 欧 美 市 场 。
The company's products mainly **target** the European and American markets.

942 阵   zhèn   **Noun:** a while; a period of time (colloquial)

guò yí zhèn wǒ men jiù néng wán chéng xiāo shòu fāng àn
过 一 阵， 我 们 就 能 完 成 销 售 方 案 。
After **a while**, we will be able to complete the sales plan.

943 争论   zhēng lùn   **Verb:** to debate; to argue **Noun:** debate; argument

Verb
wǒ tīng dào lǎo bǎn hé mì shū zài bàn gōng shì zhēng lùn
我 听 到 老 板 和 秘 书 在 办 公 室 争 论 。
I heard the boss and secretary **arguing** in the office.

Noun
tā men de zhēng lùn hǎo xiàng shì guān yú gōng zī
他 们 的 争 论 好 像 是 关 于 工 资 。
Their **argument** seemed to be about salaries.

944 征服   zhēng fú   **Verb:** to conquer

rén lèi yīng gāi bǎo hù zì rán ér bù shì zhēng fú zì rán
人 类 应 该 保 护 自 然，而 不 是 征 服 自 然 。
Humans should protect nature, not **conquer** it.

945 征求   zhēng qiú   **Verb:** to seek; to ask for

wǒ kě yǐ jiě jué zhè jiàn shì bù yòng zhēng qiú tā de
我 可 以 解 决 这 件 事， 不 用 征 求 他 的
yì jiàn
意 见 。
I can resolve this matter; there's no need **to seek** his opinion.

946 政府　　zhèng fǔ　　**Noun:** government

tīng shuō tā de qián qī hái zài **zhèng fǔ** bù mén gōng zuò
听 说 他 的 前 妻 还 在 **政府** 部 门 工 作 。
I heard that his ex-wife is still working in the **government** units.

947 政治　　zhèng zhì　　**Noun:** politics

tā jiàn guò hěn duō zhèng kè yǒu hěn qiáng de **zhèng zhì** guān diǎn
她 见 过 很 多 政 客 ， 有 很 强 的 **政治** 观 点 。
She has met a lot of politicians, and has strong **political** views.

948 之后　　zhī hòu　　later; after; afterwards

xià kè **zhī hòu** wǒ xiǎng qù tú shū guǎn jiè shū
下 课 **之后** ， 我 想 去 图 书 馆 借 书 。
After class, I want to go to the library to borrow books.

949 之间　　zhī jiān　　between; among

qí shí wǒ hé tā **zhī jiān** yǒu yì xiē máo dùn
其 实 ， 我 和 他 **之间** 有 一 些 矛 盾 。
Actually, there are some conflicts **between** me and him.

950 之前　　zhī qián　　before; prior to

zài jié hūn **zhī qián** tā duì wǒ bú gòu tǎn chéng
在 结 婚 **之前** ， 他 对 我 不 够 坦 诚 。
Before we got married, he wasn't honest enough with me.

951 之一　　zhī yī　　one of

jí tā shì wǒ zuì xǐ huān de yuè qì **zhī yī**
吉 他 是 我 最 喜 欢 的 乐 器 **之一** 。
Guitar is **one of** my favorite musical instruments.

180

952 支   zhī

Classifier for thin and long objects
Verb: to put up

Class.
tā jīn wǎn xīn qíng bù hǎo, chōu le sān zhī yān
他 今 晚 心 情 不 好, 抽 了 三 支 烟。
He was in a bad mood tonight and smoked three cigarettes.

Verb
tài hǎo le ! wǒ men zhōng yú bǎ zhàng peng zhī qǐ lái le
太 好 了 ！ 我 们 终 于 把 帐 篷 支 起 来 了。
Very good! We finally **put up** our tent.

953 植物   zhí wù

Noun: plant

wǒ men yào jiāo hái zi bǎo hù yě shēng dòng wù hé zhí wù
我 们 要 教 孩 子 保 护 野 生 动 物 和 植 物。
We need to teach children to protect wild animals and **plants**.

954 指挥   zhǐ huī

Verb: to direct; to command
Noun: command

Verb
wǒ kàn dào jiāo jǐng zài lù shàng zhǐ huī jiāo tōng
我 看 到 交 警 在 路 上 指 挥 交 通。
I saw traffic police **directing** traffic on the road.

Noun
duō shù sī jī dōu tīng cóng tā de zhǐ huī
多 数 司 机 都 听 从 他 的 指 挥。
Most drivers follow his **command**.

955 制订   zhì dìng

Verb: to formulate; to map out

wǒ xū yào zhì dìng yí fèn yè wù qǐ dòng jì huà
我 需 要 制 订 一 份 业 务 启 动 计 划。
I need to **formulate** a business launch plan.

956 质量   zhì liàng   **Noun: quality**

<ruby>厂<rt>chǎng</rt></ruby> <ruby>家<rt>jiā</rt></ruby> <ruby>保<rt>bǎo</rt></ruby> <ruby>证<rt>zhèng</rt></ruby> <ruby>了<rt>le</rt></ruby> <ruby>产<rt>chǎn</rt></ruby> <ruby>品<rt>pǐn</rt></ruby> <ruby>的<rt>de</rt></ruby> <ruby>数<rt>shù</rt></ruby> <ruby>量<rt>liàng</rt></ruby>，<ruby>却<rt>què</rt></ruby> <ruby>忽<rt>hū</rt></ruby> <ruby>略<rt>lüè</rt></ruby> <ruby>了<rt>le</rt></ruby>
<ruby>质<rt>zhì</rt></ruby> <ruby>量<rt>liàng</rt></ruby>。
Manufacturers ensured products' quantity, but ignored **quality**.

957 治   zhì   **Verb: to rule; to govern**

<ruby>州<rt>zhōu</rt></ruby> <ruby>长<rt>zhǎng</rt></ruby> <ruby>把<rt>bǎ</rt></ruby> <ruby>我<rt>wǒ</rt></ruby> <ruby>们<rt>men</rt></ruby> <ruby>的<rt>de</rt></ruby> <ruby>州<rt>zhōu</rt></ruby> <ruby>治<rt>zhì</rt></ruby> <ruby>得<rt>de</rt></ruby> <ruby>很<rt>hěn</rt></ruby> <ruby>好<rt>hǎo</rt></ruby>！
The Governor has **governed** our state well!

958 治疗   zhì liáo   **Verb: to treat (cure)** / **Noun: treatment; therapy**

Verb
<ruby>他<rt>tā</rt></ruby> <ruby>得<rt>dé</rt></ruby> <ruby>了<rt>le</rt></ruby> <ruby>癌<rt>ái</rt></ruby> <ruby>症<rt>zhèng</rt></ruby>，<ruby>最<rt>zuì</rt></ruby> <ruby>近<rt>jìn</rt></ruby> <ruby>在<rt>zài</rt></ruby> <ruby>医<rt>yī</rt></ruby> <ruby>院<rt>yuàn</rt></ruby> <ruby>治<rt>zhì</rt></ruby> <ruby>疗<rt>liáo</rt></ruby>。
He has cancer and is being **treated** in the hospital recently.

Noun
<ruby>医<rt>yī</rt></ruby> <ruby>生<rt>shēng</rt></ruby> <ruby>会<rt>huì</rt></ruby> <ruby>用<rt>yòng</rt></ruby> <ruby>放<rt>fàng</rt></ruby> <ruby>射<rt>shè</rt></ruby> <ruby>治<rt>zhì</rt></ruby> <ruby>疗<rt>liáo</rt></ruby> <ruby>为<rt>wèi</rt></ruby> <ruby>他<rt>tā</rt></ruby> <ruby>切<rt>qiē</rt></ruby> <ruby>除<rt>chú</rt></ruby> <ruby>癌<rt>ái</rt></ruby> <ruby>细<rt>xì</rt></ruby> <ruby>胞<rt>bāo</rt></ruby>。
Doctors will use radiation **therapy** to remove the cancer cells.

959 智力   zhì lì   **Noun: intelligence (of people)**

<ruby>他<rt>tā</rt></ruby> <ruby>是<rt>shì</rt></ruby> <ruby>航<rt>háng</rt></ruby> <ruby>天<rt>tiān</rt></ruby> <ruby>员<rt>yuán</rt></ruby>，**<ruby>智<rt>zhì</rt></ruby> <ruby>力<rt>lì</rt></ruby>** <ruby>肯<rt>kěn</rt></ruby> <ruby>定<rt>dìng</rt></ruby> <ruby>很<rt>hěn</rt></ruby> <ruby>高<rt>gāo</rt></ruby>。
He is an astronaut and must have a high **intelligence**.

960 智能   zhì néng   **Noun: intelligence (of artifact)**

<ruby>科<rt>kē</rt></ruby> <ruby>学<rt>xué</rt></ruby> <ruby>家<rt>jiā</rt></ruby> <ruby>们<rt>men</rt></ruby> <ruby>会<rt>huì</rt></ruby> <ruby>继<rt>jì</rt></ruby> <ruby>续<rt>xù</rt></ruby> <ruby>开<rt>kāi</rt></ruby> <ruby>发<rt>fā</rt></ruby> <ruby>人<rt>rén</rt></ruby> <ruby>工<rt>gōng</rt></ruby> <ruby>智<rt>zhì</rt></ruby> <ruby>能<rt>néng</rt></ruby>。
Scientists will continue to develop artificial **intelligence**.

961 中介　　zhōng jiè　　**Noun:** agent; intermediary

zū fáng hé mǎi fáng dōu xū yào tōng guò zhōng jiè
租 房 和 买 房 都 需 要 通 过 **中 介** 。
Both renting and buying a house need to go through an **intermediary**.

962 种类　　zhǒng lèi　　**Noun:** type; category

tā shì chú shī huì zuò bù tóng zhǒng lèi de dàn gāo
他 是 厨 师 ， 会 做 不 同 **种 类** 的 蛋 糕 。
He is a chef and can make different **types** of cakes.

963 中奖　　zhòng jiǎng　　**Verb:** to hit a jackpot

tīng shuō tā zhòng jiǎng le yíng le yì bǎi wàn měi yuán
听 说 他 **中 奖** 了 ， 赢 了 一 百 万 美 元 。
I heard that **he hit the jackpot** and won a million dollars.

964 种　　zhǒng　　**Noun:** species; type; kind

zhè zhǒng rén tài xìng yùn dà jiā dōu hěn xiàn mù tā
这 **种** 人 太 幸 运 ， 大 家 都 很 羡 慕 他 。
This **kind** of person is so lucky, everyone envies him.

965 种(植)　　zhòng zhí　　**Verb:** to plant

wǒ zài huā yuán zhòng zhí le shū cài hé guǒ shù
我 在 花 园 **种 植** 了 蔬 菜 和 果 树 。
I have **planted** vegetable and fruit trees in my garden.

966 重量　　zhòng liàng　　**Noun:** weight

zhè dài gǒu liáng de zhòng liàng shì yì qiān wǔ bǎi kè
这 袋 狗 粮 的 **重 量** 是 一 千 五 百 克 。
The **weight** of this bag of dog food is 1500 grams.

967 逐步   zhú bù   **Adverb:** step by step

wǒ yào zhú bù wán chéng wǒ de xué xí rèn wù
我 要 **逐 步** 完 成 我 的 学 习 任 务 。
I want to finish my study task **step by step**.

968 逐渐   zhú jiàn   **Adverb:** gradually

shòu tā de yǐng xiǎng wǒ zhú jiàn ài shàng le zhōng guó wén huà
受 她 的 影 响 ， 我 **逐 渐** 爱 上 了 中 国 文 化 。
Under her influence, I **gradually** fell in love with Chinese culture.

969 主题   zhǔ tí   **Noun:** theme

hěn duō zhōng shì hūn lǐ de zhǔ tí yán sè shì hóng sè
很 多 中 式 婚 礼 的 **主 题** 颜 色 是 红 色 。
Many Chinese weddings' color **theme** is red.

970 主席   zhǔ xí   **Noun:** chairman; president

zhè shì gōng sī de chuàng shǐ rén hé zhǔ xí chén xiān shēng
这 是 公 司 的 创 始 人 和 **主 席** 陈 先 生 。
This is Mr. Chen, the founder and **chairman** of the company.

971 祝福   zhù fú   **Noun:** good wishes; blessings

wǒ men hěn kāi xīn néng shōu dào jiā rén péng yǒu de zhù fú
我 们 很 开 心 能 收 到 家 人 朋 友 的 **祝 福** 。
We are happy to receive **blessings** from family and friends.

972 著名   zhù míng   **Adjective:** famous; renowned

tā shì měi guó zhù míng de zuò jiā hé qǐ yè jiā
他 是 美 国 **著 名** 的 作 家 和 企 业 家 。
He is a **renowned** author and entrepreneur in the United States.

973 著作　zhù zuò　**Noun:** book or literary composition (renowned)

wǒ shì tā de fěn sī　dú guò tā de hěn duō zhù zuò
我 是 他 的 粉 丝 ， 读 过 他 的 很 多 **著 作** 。
I am a fan of him and have read many of his **books**.

974 抓紧　zhuā jǐn　**Verb:** to grasp; to pay close attention

qǐng zhuā jǐn wǒ de shǒu　wǒ lā nǐ shàng lái
请 **抓 紧** 我 的 手 ， 我 拉 你 上 来 。
Please **grasp** my hand, I'll pull you up.

975 专心　zhuān xīn　**Verb:** to concentrate **Adverb:** attentively

Verb

tā xiǎng zhuān xīn fù xí　zàn shí bú shè jiāo
他 想 **专 心** 复 习 ， 暂 时 不 社 交 。
He wants to **concentrate** on reviewing and temporarily not socialize.

Adv.

suǒ yǐ zuì jìn tā dōu zài zhuān xīn zhǔn bèi kǎo shì ma
所 以 最 近 他 都 在 **专 心** 准 备 考 试 吗 ？
So he's been preparing for the exam **attentively** recently?

976 转动　zhuǎn dòng　**Verb:** to turn; to move

wǔ dǎo yǎn yuán men zài liàn xí zhuǎn dòng shēn tǐ
舞 蹈 演 员 们 在 练 习 **转 动** 身 体 。
The dancers are practicing **turning** their bodies.

977 转告　zhuǎn gào　**Verb:** to tell (pass on words)

qǐng nǐ zhuǎn gào tā míng tiān zǎo shàng shí diǎn lái qǔ bāo guǒ
请 你 **转 告** 他 明 天 早 上 十 点 来 取 包 裹 。
Please **tell** him to come to pick up the parcel tomorrow 10am.

978 转身   zhuǎn shēn   **Verb:** to turn; to face about

hěn qí guài, tā yí kàn dào wǒ jiù zhuǎn shēn lí kāi le
很 奇 怪，他 一 看 到 我 就 **转 身** 离 开 了。
So strange, he **turned** and left as soon as he saw me.

979 转弯   zhuǎn wān   **Verb:** to make a turn; to turn a corner

yì zhí zǒu, zài qián miàn de lù kǒu zhuǎn wān, jiù dào le
一 直 走，在 前 面 的 路 口 **转 弯**，就 到 了。
Go straight, **make a turn** at the intersection ahead, then you'll arrive.

980 转移   zhuǎn yí   **Verb:** to transfer

shén me? tā bǎ zī chǎn quán bù zhuǎn yí dào le guó wài
什 么？他 把 资 产 全 部 **转 移** 到 了 国 外？
What? He **transferred** all his assets abroad?

981 装修   zhuāng xiū   **Verb:** to renovate

wǒ dǎ suàn nián dǐ zhuāng xiū wǒ men de gōng yù
我 打 算 年 底 **装 修** 我 们 的 公 寓。
I plan to **renovate** our apartment at the end of the year.

982 装置   zhuāng zhì   **Noun:** device; installation

jì shù xué yuàn de diàn nǎo zhuāng zhì yǒu diǎn luò hòu
技 术 学 院 的 电 脑 **装 置** 有 点 落 后。
The computer **installations** in the Technical College are a bit outdated.

983 追求　　　　zhuī qiú　　　**Verb:** to pursue
Noun: pursuit

Verb
tā nián qīng de shí hòu　　yǒu hěn duō nǚ shēng zhuī qiú tā
他 年 轻 的 时 候， 有 很 多 女 生 **追 求** 他。
When he was young, many girls **pursued** him.

Noun
tā hěn jiāo ào　　dāng rán méi yǒu jiē shòu tā men de zhuī qiú
他 很 骄 傲， 当 然 没 有 接 受 她 们 的 **追 求**。
He was very proud, of course did not accept their **pursuit**.

---

984 准时　　　　zhǔn shí　　　**Adjective:** on time

wǒ men yuē hǎo míng tiān　　diǎn zài kā fēi guǎn zhǔn shí
我 们 约 好 明 天 12 点 在 咖 啡 馆 **准 时**
jiàn miàn
见 面。
We agreed to meet **on time** at the coffee shop tomorrow at 12pm.

---

985 资料　　　　zī liào　　　**Noun:** material

tā men zài wǎng shàng gòu mǎi le yí tào xué xí zī liào
他 们 在 网 上 购 买 了 一 套 学 习 **资 料**。
They purchased a set of learning **materials** online.

---

986 资源　　　　zī yuán　　　**Noun:** resources

zhè gè wǎng zhàn shàng yǒu hěn duō yǒu yòng de xué xí zī yuán
这 个 网 站 上 有 很 多 有 用 的 学 习 **资 源**。
There are many useful learning **resources** on this site.

987 自　　　　zì

Preposition: from; since
Pronoun: self; oneself

Pre.
zhè gè hé tong zì jīn tiān qǐ shēng xiào
这 个 合 同 **自** 今 天 起 生 效 。
This contract is effective **from** today.

Pro.
zhè gè yì wàn fù wēng pò chǎn hòu jiù zì shā le
这 个 亿 万 富 翁 破 产 后 ， 就 **自** 杀 了 。
After the billionaire went bankrupt, he took his own life (**self**-kill).

988 自信　　　　zì xìn

Adjective: confident
Noun: confidence

Verb
zhè gè bó zhǔ bú shì zì xìn ér shì zì dà
这 个 博 主 不 是 **自** **信** ， 而 是 自 大 ！
This blogger is not **confident**, but arrogant!

Noun
tā xū yào de shì qiān xū hé zhēn zhèng de zì xìn
他 需 要 的 是 谦 虚 和 真 正 的 **自** **信** 。
What he needs is humility and true **confidence**.

989 字母　　　　zì mǔ

Noun: alphabet; letters

xué huì pīn yīn zì mǔ jiù kě yǐ yòng pīn yīn dǎ zì
学 会 拼 音 **字** **母** ， 就 可 以 用 拼 音 打 字 。
Once you learn the pinyin **alphabet**, you can type with pinyin.

990 综合　　　　zōng hé

Adjective: comprehensive

wǒ fā xiàn shì chǎng shàng de hěn duō zōng hé jiào cái hěn
我 发 现 市 场 上 的 很 多 **综** **合** 教 材 很
kū zào
枯 燥 。
I find many **comprehensive** textbooks on the market boring.

991 总共   zǒng gòng   **Adverb:** in total

běi yuē fēng huì shàng zǒng gòng yǒu duō shǎo gè guó jiā lǐng dǎo
北 约 峰 会 上 **总 共** 有 多 少 个 国 家 领 导 ?
How many country leaders are there **in total** at the NATO summit?

992 总理   zǒng lǐ   **Noun:** chancellor; premier

dé guó zǒng lǐ huì qīn zì jiē jiàn zhōng guó zhǔ xí
德 国 **总 理** 会 亲 自 接 见 中 国 主 席 。
The German **chancellor** will personally receive the Chinese president.

993 总统   zǒng tǒng   **Noun:** president (of a republic country)

měi guó zǒng tǒng hé yīng guó shǒu xiàng yě huì zài chǎng
美 国 **总 统** 和 英 国 首 相 也 会 在 场 。
The **President** of USA and the Prime Minister of the UK will also be present.

994 总之   zǒng zhī   **Conjunction:** in a word; in conclusion

zǒng zhī hěn duō lǐng dǎo cān jiā le rén dào zhǔ yì fēng huì
总 之 , 很 多 领 导 参 加 了 人 道 主 义 峰 会 。
In conclusion, many leaders participated in the humanitarian summit.

995 阻止   zǔ zhǐ   **Verb:** to prevent

huì yì de zōng zhǐ shì zǔ zhǐ rén quán de qīn fàn
会 议 的 宗 旨 是 **阻 止** 人 权 的 侵 犯 。
The conference aims **to prevent** human rights abuses.

996 嘴(巴)   zuǐ ba   **Noun:** mouth

tā zuǐ ba chòu suǒ yǐ tā jù jué hé tā jiē wěn
他 嘴 巴 臭， 所 以 她 拒 绝 和 他 接 吻。
His **mouth** smells, so she refuses to kiss him.

997 最初   zuì chū   **Noun:** initial; first

zuì chū wǒ xiǎng jì xù róng rěn tā dàn tài nán le
最 初 我 想 继 续 容 忍 他， 但 太 难 了。
At first I wanted to keep tolerating him, but it's so hard.

998 作出   zuò chū   **Verb:** to make (choice, decision)

zhè shì wǒ rèn zhēn sī kǎo hòu zuò chū de jué dìng
这 是 我 认 真 思 考 后 作 出 的 决 定。
This is a decision I **made** after careful consideration.

999 作为   zuò wéi   **Verb:** to regard as; to take as
Noun: deeds; achievement

Verb

zuò wéi nǐ de hǎo yǒu wǒ wèi nǐ de jué dìng gāo xìng
作 为 你 的 好 友， 我 为 你 的 决 定 高 兴。
As your friend, I am happy for your decision.

Noun

tā suī rán yǒu bó shì xué wèi què méi yǒu zuò wéi
他 虽 然 有 博 士 学 位， 却 没 有 作 为。
Although he has a doctorate, he has no **achievement**.

1000 做梦   zuò mèng   **Verb:** to dream (in sleep or illusion)

wǒ zuó wǎn zuò mèng huí dào le xiǎo shí hòu de jiā
我 昨 晚 做 梦 回 到 了 小 时 候 的 家。
I **dreamt** last night that I went back to my childhood home.

2

KEY GRAMMAR

IN CONTEXT

① 只要...就...

zhǐ yào　　　　　　　　　　jiù
只 要 + condition + 就 + result

to express a conditional statement
as long as... then...

Ex. 1

zhǐ yào nǐ bàn shì chéng gōng　　jiù néng shēng zhí
只 要 你 办 事 成 功 , 就 能 升 职 。

As long as you succeed in handling the matter, (**then**) you will be promoted.

Ex. 2

zhǐ yào nǐ dá yìng bǎo mì ,　wǒ men jiù bú huì
只 要 你 答 应 保 密 , 我 们 就 不 会
yǒu máo dùn
有 矛 盾 。

As long as you promise to keep it secret, **then** we won't have any conflicts.

Write your own:

② 虽然...但(是)...

suī rán　　　　　　　dàn shì
虽 然 + clause 1 + 但(是)+ clause 2

to express contrast or contradiction
although... (but)...

Ex. 1

suī rán tā de jiào yù bèi jǐng hǎo ,　dàn shì gōng
虽 然 他 的 教 育 背 景 好 , 但 是 工
zuò néng lì ruò
作 能 力 弱 。

Although his educational background is good, (**but**) his work ability is weak.

Ex. 2

tā suī rán shì bǎi wàn fù wēng ,　dàn hěn lìn sè
他 虽 然 是 百 万 富 翁 , 但 很 吝 啬 。

Although he is a millionaire, (**but**) he is very stingy.

Write your own:

③ 在...的...下

zài
在 + someone + 的 + noun + clause
de

to describe a specific condition under which something takes place or exists
under/with/via...

Ex. 1

zài fù mǔ de zhī chí xià　　tā hé nán yǒu dìng hūn le
在父母的支持下，她和男友订婚了。
With the support of her parents, she got engaged to her boyfriend.

Ex. 2

zài jiào shòu de tuī jiàn xià，　tā dào le dà xué
在教授的推荐下，他到了大学
shí xí
实习。
With the professor's recommendation, he took an internship at the university.

Write your own:

④ ...不重要，重要的是...

bú zhòng yào　zhòng yào de shì
A + **不重要，重要的是** + B

to emphasize the importance of one aspect while downplaying another
...doesn't matter, what matters is...

Ex. 1

cái fù bú zhòng yào　zhòng yào de shì jiàn kāng hé kuài lè
财富不重要，重要的是健康和快乐。
Wealth **doesn't matter**, **what matters is** health and happiness.

Ex. 2

chǎn pǐn de yán sè bú zhòng yào　zhòng yào de shì zhì liàng
产品的颜色不重要，重要的是质量。
The color of the product **doesn't matter**, **what matters is** the quality.

Write your own:

⑤ 什么...都...

subject + 什么 (shén me) + (noun) + 都 (dōu) + verb	to convey inclusiveness or universality **anything / anyone**

Ex. 1

tā hěn shēng qì　　shén me huà dōu bù shuō
他 很 生 气，**什 么** 话 **都** 不 说。
He was very angry and didn't say **anything**.

Ex. 2

shén me rén dōu kě yǐ cān jiā zhè gè huó dòng
什 么 人 **都** 可 以 参 加 这 个 活 动。
Anyone can participate in this event.

Write your own:

⑥ 什么...就...

verb + 什么 (shén me) + 就 (jiù) + verb + (什么) (shén me)	to convey an immediate or conditional response or action **whenever/whatever... then...**

Ex. 1

zhè lǐ de fàn cài　　nǐ xiǎng chī shén me　　jiù chī
这 里 的 饭 菜，你 想 吃 **什 么**，**就** 吃。
For the food here, you can eat **whatever** you want.

Ex. 2

zhè shì gōng gòng chǎng hé　　bù néng xiǎng zuò shén me jiù
这 是 公 共 场 合，不 能 想 做 **什 么 就**
zuò shén me
做 **什 么**。
This is a public place, you can't do **whatever** you want.

Write your own:

194

⑦ 向...学(习)...

A + 向 + B + 学(习)
xiàng · xué · xí

to learn from / be instructed by

Ex. 1

关 于 当 地 文 化 ， 我 们 要 向 导 游
guān yú dāng dì wén huà · wǒ men yào xiàng dǎo yóu
学 习 。
xué xí

Regarding local culture, we have **to learn from** the tour guide.

Ex. 2

新 手 们 在 向 王 经 理 学 卖 车 。
xīn shǒu men zài xiàng wáng jīng lǐ xué mài chē

The novices are **learning from** Manager Wang about selling cars.

Write your own:

⑧ 没想到...

(subject) + 没 想 到 + clause
méi xiǎng dào

to express surprise or an unexpected outcome
unexpectedly / didn't expect...

Ex. 1

我 没 想 到 他 居 然 从 来 没 有 真
wǒ méi xiǎng dào tā jū rán cóng lái méi yǒu zhēn
心 爱 过 我 。
xīn ài guò wǒ

I **didn't expect** that he actually never truly loved me.

Ex. 2

没 想 到 陈 主 管 也 被 老 板 炒 了 。
méi xiǎng dào chén zhǔ guǎn yě bèi lǎo bǎn chǎo le

Unexpectedly, Director Chen is also fired by the boss.

Write your own:

195

⑨ 除了...还/都...

除了 +A+ **还/都** +B
<small>chú le　　hái dōu</small>

to indicate that in addition to one thing, there is another thing or action **except/ apart from/ besides...**

Ex. 1

<small>chú le tiào wǔ　　tā hái xǐ huān dǎ wǎng qiú</small>
除了跳舞，她**还**喜欢打网球。

Besides dancing, she **also** enjoys playing tennis

Ex. 2

<small>chú le wǒ　dà jiā dōu bú huì yòng zhè gè chéng xù</small>
除了我，大家**都**不会用这个程序。

Apart from me, no one is able to use this program.

Write your own:

⑩ 宁愿...也...

subject + **宁愿** + verb 1 + **也** + verb 2
<small>níng yuàn　　yě</small>

to express a preference for one option or choice over another **rather... than...**

Ex. 1

<small>tā tài lǎn　　níng yuàn shuì jiào　　yě bù yuàn gōng zuò</small>
他太懒，**宁愿**睡觉，**也**不愿工作。

He is too lazy and would **rather** sleep **than** work.

Ex. 2

<small>wǒ níng yuàn dān shēn　　yě bù xiǎng hé tā nà yàng</small>
我**宁愿**单身，**也**不想和他那样
<small>de rén jiāo wǎng</small>
的人交往。

I would **rather** be single **than** date someone like him.

Write your own:

196

⑪ 就算...也...

jiù suàn
就 算 + condition + 也 + result
yě

even if... still
(stronger/assertive tone)

Ex. 1

jiù suàn gōng sī de dài yù biàn hǎo wǒ yě yào
就 算 公 司 的 待 遇 变 好 ， 我 也 要
cí zhí
辞 职 。

Even if the company's treatment improves, I **still** want to resign.

Ex. 2

jiù suàn méi yǒu háo huá de hūn lǐ wǒ yě yuàn
就 算 没 有 豪 华 的 婚 礼 ， 我 也 愿
yì hé tā jié hūn
意 和 他 结 婚 。

Even if there's no extravagant wedding, I'm **still** willing to marry him.

Write your own:

⑫ 即使...也...

jí shǐ
即 使 + condition + 也 + result
yě

even if... still...
(weaker/more formal tone)

Ex. 1

jí shǐ chuàng yè shī bài wǒ yě bú huì hòu huǐ
即 使 创 业 失 败 ， 我 也 不 会 后 悔 。

Even if my entrepreneurial venture fails, I will **still** not regret it.

Ex. 2

jí shǐ shǒu shù chéng gōng tā de jiàn kāng yě wú
即 使 手 术 成 功 ， 她 的 健 康 也 无
fǎ wán quán huī fù
法 完 全 恢 复 。

Even if the surgery is successful, her health **still** cannot fully recover.

Write your own:

⑬ 难道...

| nán dào
难 道 + question | to form rhetorical question |

Ex. 1

tā tiān tiān mà nǐ, nán dào nǐ yào yǒng yuǎn rěn ma
他 天 天 骂 你，**难 道** 你 要 永 远 忍 吗？

He scolds you every day, are you going to endure it forever?

Ex. 2

xiàn zài shì líng xià sān dù, nǐ nán dào bù lěng ma
现 在 是 零 下 三 度，你 **难 道** 不 冷 吗？

It's minus three degrees now, aren't you cold?

Write your own:

⑭ 一旦...就...

| yí dàn
一 旦 + condition + jiù
就 + result | to describe a cause-and-effect relationship between conditions or events
once... (then) |

Ex. 1

yí dàn huò qǔ qíng bào, jiù mǎ shàng lí kāi
一 旦 获 取 情 报，**就** 马 上 离 开。

Once you obtain the intelligence, **then** leave immediately.

Ex. 2

yí dàn xià yǔ, wǒ men jiù děi fàng qì yě cān
一 旦 下 雨，我 们 **就** 得 放 弃 野 餐
jì huà
计 划。

Once it rains, **then** we have to abandon the picnic plan.

Write your own:

⑮ 随着...

^{suí} ^{zhe}
随 着 + condition + result

to show that something is happening with or in response to another event
as... (something happens)

Ex. 1
^{suí} ^{zhe} ^{jià} ^{gé} ^{shàng} ^{zhǎng} ^{yuè} ^{lái} ^{yuè} ^{duō} ^{de} ^{rén}
随 着 价 格 上 涨， 越 来 越 多 的 人
^{huì} ^{tíng} ^{zhǐ} ^{gòu} ^{mǎi}
会 停 止 购 买 。
As prices rise, more and more people will stop buying.

Ex. 2
^{suí} ^{zhe} ^{ái} ^{xì} ^{bāo} ^{de} ^{kuò} ^{sàn} ^{tā} ^{de} ^{bìng} ^{qíng}
随 着 癌 细 胞 的 扩 散， 他 的 病 情
^{gèng} ^{zāo} ^{gāo} ^{le}
更 糟 糕 了 。
As the cancer cells spread, his condition worsens.

Write your own:

⑯ 连...都 / 也...

^{lián} ^{dōu} ^{yě}
连 + subject + **都 / 也** + statement

to emphasize that something includes even the most extreme element
even...

Ex. 1
^{tā} ^{tài} ^{gù} ^{zhí} ^{lián} ^{tā} ^{bà} ^{yě} ^{bù} ^{néng} ^{shuō} ^{fú} ^{tā}
他 太 固 执，连 他 爸 也 不 能 说 服 他 。
He is too stubborn, **even** his dad can't persuade him.

Ex. 2
^{nǎi} ^{nai} ^{yǒu} ^{lǎo} ^{nián} ^{chī} ^{dāi} ^{zhèng} ^{lián} ^{chī} ^{fàn} ^{dōu}
奶 奶 有 老 年 痴 呆 症，连 吃 饭 都
^{yào} ^{wǒ} ^{tí} ^{xǐng}
要 我 提 醒 。
My grandma has dementia, I need to remind her **even** to eat.

Write your own:

⑰ 虽然...却...

suī rán
虽 然 + clause 1 + 却 + clause 2
què

to express a contrast or contradiction
between two parts of a statement
although... but/yet

Ex. 1

zhè gè fāng àn suī rán fù zá, què kě yǐ tí
这 个 方 案 虽 然 复 杂， 却 可 以 提
gāo gōng zuò xiào lǜ
高 工 作 效 率 。
Although this scheme is complicated, (**but**) it can improve work efficiency.

Ex. 2

tā suī rán bú ài tā, què bù tóng yì hé tā
他 虽 然 不 爱 她， 却 不 同 意 和 她
lí hūn
离 婚 。
Even though he doesn't love her, (**yet**) he doesn't agree to divorce her.

Write your own:

⑱ 和...保持/断绝联系

hé bǎo chí duàn jué lián xì
A + 和 + B + 保 持 / 断 绝 联 系

to keep/cut off contact with...

Ex. 1

bì yè hòu, wǒ réng rán hé tóng xué men bǎo chí lián xì
毕 业 后，我 仍 然 和 同 学 们 保 持 联 系 。
After graduation, I still **keep in touch with** my classmates.

Ex. 2

lǎo zhāng lí zhí hòu, jiù hé wǒ men duàn jué le lián xì
老 张 离 职 后， 就 和 我 们 断 绝 了 联 系 。
After Lao Zhang resigned, he **cut off contact with** us.

Write your own:

200

shì   zhī   yī
subject + 是 + noun + 之 一

to indicate that something is "one of" a group or a set of items

Ex. 1

tā shì wǒ men bù mén zuì yōu xiù de gōng chéng
他 是 我 们 部 门 最 优 秀 的 工 程
shī zhī yī
师 之 一 。

He is **one of the** most excellent engineers in our department.

Ex. 2

zhè gè gōng sī shì wǒ men jié mù zuì dà de
这 个 公 司 是 我 们 节 目 最 大 的
zàn zhù shāng zhī yī
赞 助 商 之 一 。

This company is **one of the** largest sponsors of our program.

Write your own:

jì bù   yě bù
既 不 + feature 1 + 也 不 + feature 2

to express that something is neither one thing nor another
neither... nor...

Ex. 1

wǒ de rì cháng shēng huó jì bù wú liáo , yě bù
我 的 日 常 生 活 既 不 无 聊 ， 也 不
jīng cǎi
精 彩 。

My daily life is **neither** boring **nor** exciting.

Ex. 2

tā jì bù dào qiàn , yě bù jiě shì , zhēn fán
他 既 不 道 歉 ， 也 不 解 释 ， 真 烦 ！

He **neither** apologizes **nor** explains, so annoying!

Write your own:

ACCESS AUDIO

Please follow the instructions provided below to access the Chinese audio for this book:

INSTRUCTIONS TO ACCESS AUDIO

1. **Scan this QR code**
   or go to: **www.linglingmandarin.com/books**

2. Locate this book in the list of LingLing Mandarin Books

3. Click the "Access Audio" button

   Access Audio

4. Enter the password:

AWB33

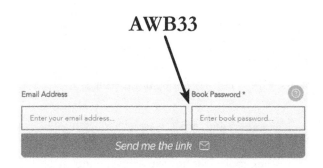

NEW HSK VOCABULARY SERIES

LEARN CHINESE
VOCABULARY FOR
BEGINNERS:
NEW HSK 1

LEARN CHINESE
VOCABULARY FOR
BEGINNERS:
NEW HSK 2

LEARN CHINESE
VOCABULARY FOR
BEGINNERS:
NEW HSK 3

LEARN CHINESE
VOCABULARY FOR
INTERMEDIATE:
NEW HSK 4

LEARN CHINESE
VOCABULARY FOR
INTERMEDIATE:
NEW HSK 5

LEARN CHINESE
VOCABULARY FOR
INTERMEDIATE:
NEW HSK 6

Get notified about **new releases**
https://linglingmandarin.com/notify

BOOKS BY LINGLING

CHINESE CONVERSATIONS
FOR BEGINNERS

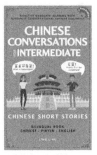

CHINESE CONVERSATIONS
FOR INTERMEDIATE

MANDARIN WRITING
PRACTICE BOOK

CHINESE STORIES
FOR LANGUAGE LEARNERS:
ELEMENTARY

CHINESE STORIES
FOR LANGUAGE LEARNERS:
INTERMEDIATE

THE ART OF WAR
FOR LANGUAGE LEARNERS

Get notified about **new releases**
https://linglingmandarin.com/notify

ABOUT THE AUTHOR

LingLing is a native Chinese Mandarin educator with an MA in Communication and Language. Originally from China, now living in the UK, she is the founder of the learning brand LingLing Mandarin, which aims to create the best resources for learners to master the Chinese language and achieve deep insight into Chinese culture in a fun and illuminating way. *Discover more about LingLing and access more great resources by following the links below or scanning the QR codes.*

 WEBSITE
linglingmandarin.com

YOUTUBE
youtube.com/c/linglingmandarin

 PATREON
patreon.com/linglingmandarin

INSTAGRAM
instagram.com/linglingmandarin

Made in the USA
Las Vegas, NV
14 October 2024

96863922R00118